Jewish Beliefs and Practices

Jan Thompson

Edward Arnold

© Jan Thompson 1983

First published 1983 by
Edward Arnold (Publishers) Ltd
41 Bedford Square, London WC1B 3DQ

British Library Cataloguing in Publication Data

Thompson, Jan
    Jewish Belief and Practice
    1. Judaism
    I. Title
    296   BM561

    ISBN 0-7131-0875-4

Acknowledgements

The publisher wishes to thank the following for permission to
reproduce copyright material:
    New English Bible second edition © 1970 by permission of Oxford
and Cambridge University Presses.
The publisher would also like to thank the following for their
permission to use copyright illustrations:
    BIPAC: figs. 2, 4 &-14; Juliette Soester MMPA: figs. 3, 7, 10 &
12; Mansell Collection: fig. 6; David Richardson: figs. 8 & 9;
Jan Thompson: fig. 11; Popperfoto: fig. 13.

Dedication

To my father
and in loving memory of my mother.
'The Lord bless you and keep you.'

Printed in Great Britain by
Thomson Litho Ltd, East Kilbride, Scotland

Contents

Preface

This book is another in a series on world religions, written for the more able pupils of 14 years and upwards. It presents a summary of Judaism, assuming no previous knowledge on the part of the reader, so that everything is explained. Yet it includes a considerable amount of detail which one would not normally find in introductions to a religion, but which is often sought for by this age group and required for a serious study of the subject. This is particularly important with Judaism since the Jews themselves can express a deep concern with even the smallest details in their effort to live their lives in accordance with God's instructions. My main aim, however, is not just to give facts but always to explore the meaning and significance they hold for their adherents so that we might come to a deeper understanding of that religion.

In my previous books on Christianity and Islam, the figures of Jesus and Muhammad respectively formed the framework. I have used this device to some extent here, starting a number of chapters with Moses; but generally speaking this format has been less easy to apply to Judaism as historical events throughout the ages have shaped the Jewish religion. The fact that Jews are bound together by their sense of a shared history, relived regularly in their festivals, has led me to give greater emphasis in this book to the historical development of the religion and to the Jewish festivals.

Judaism has often been studied simply as background knowledge for understanding Christianity and some people have only come across the very one-sided picture of Judaism in the New Testament. Many pupils of Christian background do not realise that it is a living religion which has continued to develop into the present day. It is hoped that this book will help to correct such impressions.

1 The Jews

Judaism is one of the oldest of the world's living religions and it has always been one of the smallest. Its followers are called Jews and there are about 15 million of them. Their number was considerably reduced in the 20th century when 6 million were put to death under Hitler in the Second World War. This Holocaust is but one great tragedy in their history of persecution and survival against all odds. Most of them live in Jewish communities scattered all over the world: 5½ million in the USA and many in Russia and Europe. In 1948 CE (common era – equivalent date to AD) the State of Israel was established as the Jewish homeland (see Fig. 1), with Jerusalem as its capital city and its citizens known as Israelis. This was set up in the Middle East, in the area where their ancestors had lived and which they have always regarded as their Promised Land. Israel is a unifying factor for Jews throughout the world: they feel deeply patriotic towards it and many have emigrated there so that there are now over 3 million Jews in this new country.

The word 'Jew' comes from Judah, one of the earliest fathers of this people who gave his name to the ancient Jewish kingdom centred on Jerusalem. They were not always called Jews, a name which first appears in the Bible in Jeremiah 32 verse 12, that is in the 7th century BCE (before the common era – equivalent date to BC). Before this they were known as Israelites, or the Children of Israel, and earlier still as Hebrews. We shall simply use the term 'Jews' for them, whatever the period. The Jews trace their ancestry back to Abraham who probably lived about 1800 BCE and who, through his son Isaac and his grandson Jacob, became the father of a tribe. Abraham is believed to have come from a region in present day Iraq and to have been led by the one God to the country where Israel is today (at that time it was known as Canaan, and later as Palestine). The Jewish holy book, the Hebrew Bible (which is the same as the Christian Old Testament), records how God said to Abraham:

> Leave your country, your kinsmen, and your father's house, and go to a country that I will show you. I will make you into a great nation, I will bless you and make your name so great that it shall be used in blessings.
> (*Genesis 12 verses 1-2*)

1

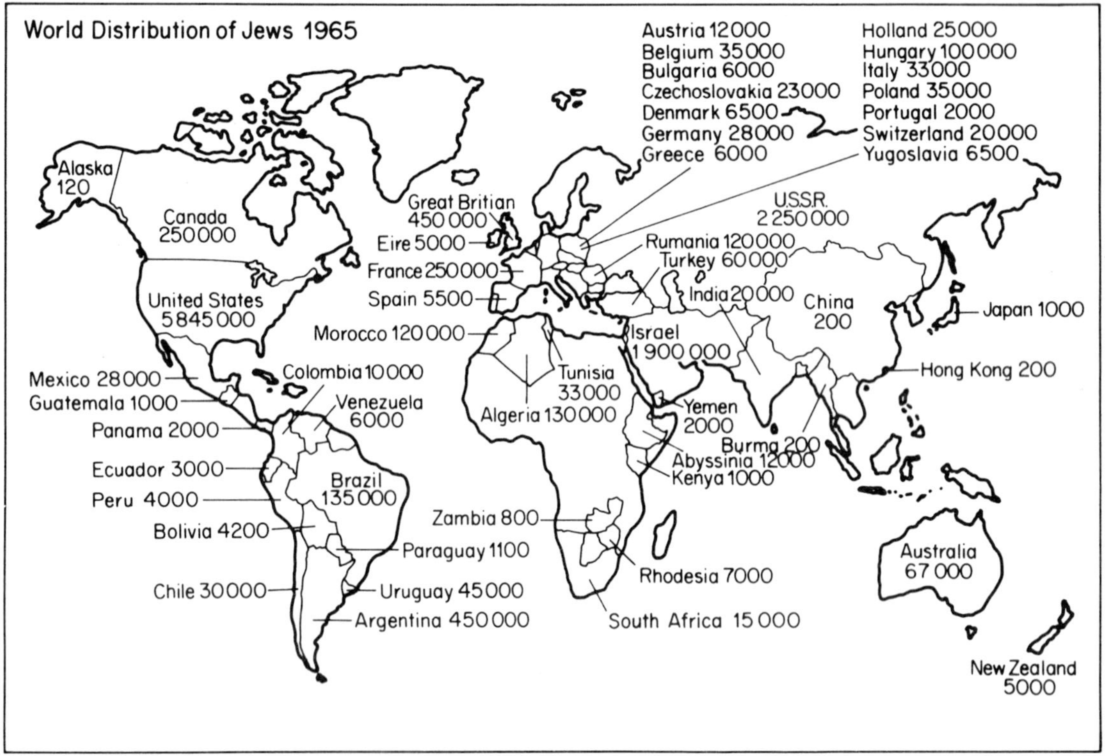

World Distribution of Jews 1965

Alaska	120
Canada	250000
United States	5845000
Mexico	28000
Guatemala	1000
Panama	2000
Colombia	10000
Venezuela	6000
Ecuador	3000
Peru	4000
Bolivia	4200
Brazil	135000
Paraguay	1100
Uruguay	45000
Chile	30000
Argentina	450000
Great Britian	450000
Eire	5000
France	250000
Spain	5500
Morocco	120000
Algeria	130000
Tunisia	33000
Austria	12000
Belgium	35000
Bulgaria	6000
Czechoslovakia	23000
Denmark	6500
Germany	28000
Greece	6000
Holland	25000
Hungary	100000
Italy	33000
Poland	35000
Portugal	2000
Switzerland	20000
Yugoslavia	6500
USSR	2250000
Rumania	120000
Turkey	60000
Israel	1900000
Yemen	2000
India	20000
Abyssinia	12000
Kenya	1000
Burma	200
China	200
Japan	1000
Hong Kong	200
Rhodesia	7000
Zambia	800
South Africa	15000
Australia	67000
New Zealand	5000

Fig. 1 World distribution of Jews (1965).

2

Yet it is not to Abraham that we look for the founder of Judaism. If we wanted to identify one person as being most influential in shaping this religion it would be Moses, who probably lived about 1300 BCE. It was Moses, the law-giver, who gave the Jews a sense of identity as the People of God and who laid the foundations of the social, ceremonial and legal systems of Judaism. Nevertheless it is more accurate to say that there is no single human founder of Judaism. It has been shaped through the ages by individual men and women and by historical events; and this process has gone on beyond biblical times so that a knowledge of the Bible alone is not enough for an understanding of this religion.

The tribal nature of the Jews continues to this day in that they are a group of people mostly related to each other by blood ties. They are not a separate race and the features so often attributed to Jews are common to many people of the Middle East. Strictly speaking, a Jew or Jewess is someone who has been born of a Jewish mother and who has not renounced his or her religion for another. There are also a small minority of Jews who have converted to this religion.

Jewish identity is strengthened by their sense of a shared history and a shared destiny as God's chosen people. They regard themselves as his holy nation whose responsibility and privilege it is to fulfil the many laws that God has laid upon them. These laws affect every part of their life, not just their more obviously religious beliefs and practices, but their whole moral outlook and way of life, even down to the food they eat. It is possible therefore to find non-believing Jews who do not attend religious services and yet still regard themselves as Jewish because they identify with their Jewish family and culture. Judaism does not emphasize personal conversion and acceptance of beliefs so much as the Jew's duty to respond to God within the group. Nevertheless, this book must concern itself with fully practising Jews.

There are various groups within Judaism. The differences between the Sephardim and the Ashkenazim stem mainly from the fact that they have developed separately in different areas from at least the Middle Ages. Sephardi Jews originated from Spain and Portugal and Ashkenazi Jews from the rest of Europe, although both spread further afield. There are cultural and religious differences between them but modern Israel is succeeding in merging the two groups into one nation and intermarriage between them is quite acceptable to both sides.

A more serious rift exists between traditional Judaism and some recent modernising trends. Orthodox Jews are in the majority in all countries except the USA and Canada. They want to continue the old traditions, based on their Bible and the Jewish teachings of the first few centuries CE. Orthodox Jewry has various sub-groups within it, like the Ultra-Orthodox Jews, conspicuous by their

3

appearance which derives from their past in Eastern Europe. They have short hair except for their long side curls and beards, black wide-brimmed hats or round fur-edged ones, black coats down to their knees, black trousers and white shirts without ties (see Fig. 11).

Since the end of the 18th century a Progressive movement has developed to modernise Judaism and help the Jew to be accepted in gentile society. Progressive Jews follow Conservative, Reform and Liberal Judaism, in increasing degrees of modernism. They want to retain the essential principles of biblical Judaism but to reinterpret and reapply them in the modern world. They claim that a living religion should make *progress*, relying on God's continued inspiration, and should not be hampered by rigid, old-fashioned codes of practice which have long since lost their meaning. Some examples of how these differences affect them in practice will be pointed out in the course of this book, but basically they are far less restricted by the minor details in all areas of Jewish law, and also feel free to introduce new practices like allowing women to play a more active part in the synagogues.

Make sure you know
1 who was the first father of the Jews
2 who was the most important leader of the Jews
3 the name given to western Jews, i.e. those from most parts of Europe.

See if you understand
4 why the followers of this religion are called Jews
5 who can claim to be Jewish
6 the basic difference of outlook between Orthodox and Progressive Jews

Further assignment
7 Study the history chart and pick out the references to Abraham, Isaac, Jacob, Judah and Moses (all mentioned in this chapter).

History chart

Approximate dates
BCE (before common era)

1800	Abraham left Mesopotamia for Canaan
1700	His son Isaac and grandson Jacob (also called Israel) in Canaan
1600	Jacob's fourth son was Judah; Hebrews settled in Egypt
1500	Hebrews enslaved in Egypt
1300	Exodus from Egypt under Moses; Wilderness Period
1100	Settlement in Canaan/Palestine
1000	Monarchy: Kings Saul, David and Solomon
900	Kingdom split into Judah in south and Israel in north (922)
800	Prophets Amos and Hosea
700	Prophets Isaiah of Jerusalem and Micah; Assyrians conquered Israel (722)
600	Prophet Jeremiah; Babylonians conquered Judah and Temple destroyed; Exile and beginning of Dispersion (586); Prophet Ezekiel
500	Prophet Isaiah II; Second Temple built
300	Under Greek Empire
150	Maccabean Revolt against foreign influences (167); Hasmonean Dynasty
50	Under Roman Empire

CE (common era)

50	Great Revolt, Temple destroyed (70), last stand at Masada
150	Bar Kochba Revolt, Jerusalem made into a pagan city (135), Dispersion
1900	Zionist movement Holocaust; State of Israel established (1948)

2 The Jewish calendar

Jews celebrate many annual festivals, as well as those which mark important stages in their lives. They prepare carefully beforehand for each festival so that their homes are clean and tidy and they themselves are washed and dressed in their best clothes. These are usually times for giving presents and remembering the poor. A special festive meal is always served which begins with blessings said in Hebrew over a pair of candles, a goblet of wine and two special, plaited loaves of bread, all symbols of rejoicing and plenty. The wine and bread are shared round before the proper meal is eaten.

Festivals are important for deepening the Jews' sense of identity as they meet together around the family meal table or in the local synagogue to relive their history. All the major festivals are described in this book, usually at the end of each chapter. Not all Jewish festivals are Holy Days in the strict sense of being holidays on which no unnecessary work should be done, but only those laid down in their most important scriptures, the Torah, and then not always for the entire length of the festival. To understand them better you need to know something about the Jewish calendar and to refer to the festival chart on page 9.

Jewish days begin at sunset, not midnight. This practice comes from the Creation story in chapter 1 of the biblical book of Genesis where each section ends: 'So evening came, and morning came, the first day' (or 'a second day' etc.). The day lasts 24 hours but festival days, like Sabbaths, are extended to 25 hours because it is not certain whether the period between sunset and nightfall should be regarded as the end of one day or the beginning of the next; so they take the longer period to avoid breaking the rules of the festival.

The week has seven days. These are not given names in Hebrew but simply known as 'First Day' (Sunday) etc. to 'Sixth Day' or 'Sabbath Eve' (Friday) and 'Sabbath' (Saturday). Sabbath is the last and most important day of the week. It is a weekly festival, a holy day during which work is forbidden. The Sabbath is always observed even when it occurs during another, annual festival like Tabernacles. Some other festivals are moved if their date falls on the Sabbath (see Independence Day and 9th Av in the chart on page 9).

Fig. 2   The festival of Purim, celebrated in Israel. Mordecai, the hero and saviour of the Jewish people, is pictured seated on a white horse. (See chapter 12.)

The Jewish months are calculated by the movement of the moon rather than the sun. These lunar months begin with the new moon and last either 29 or 30 days since the moon takes about 29½ days to circle the earth. The Jewish year, in contrast, is solar rather than lunar, since the annual festivals correspond to the agricultural seasons (e.g. Passover is a spring festival, originally connected with the beginning of the barley harvest). The lunar year is 11 days shorter than the solar year so the calendar has to be adjusted by fitting in an extra month seven times every 19 years on the 3rd, 6th, 8th, 11th, 14th, 17th and 19th year in each cycle. In these 'leap' years the extra month follows Adar and is called Adar Sheni (Second Adar). In such a year the festival of Purim falls on the 14th day of the extra month rather than in Adar.

The Jewish year can be said to start at two places: 1st Nisan which comes at the beginning of spring and 1st Tishre which comes at the beginning of autumn. In a passage on the Passover which falls in the month of Nisan, the Bible says:

This month is for you the first of months; you shall make it the first month of the year. (*Exodus 12 verse 2*)

Yet 1st Tishre is when the New Year Festival is celebrated. This is not so strange when you remember that we have different times to start the school year and the financial year and so on. 1981-1982 CE was the year 5742 for the Jews, which is traditionally calculated to be the age of the world from its creation by God. Modern Jews, however, understand this as referring to the birth of civilisation rather than of the world.

Make sure you know
1 the name of at least one Holy Day of rest, apart from the Sabbath (see festival chart)
2 when a Jewish day starts
3 which is the first day of the Jewish week

See if you understand
4 how a Jew would refer to a Wednesday (morning)
5 why it is necessary to have an extra month in certain years
6 why Jews could think of the New Year starting at two different times in the year

Issues to discuss
7 How can festivals strengthen Judaism?
8 Which important stages in life are often marked by a special ceremony? (These are known as life-cycle rituals.) Why do people generally think it is important to celebrate them, often going to great trouble and expense to do so, and gathering family and friends from afar?

Hebrew months	Western equivalents	Dates	Major annual festivals
Tishre	September-October	*1st (*1st – *2nd for Orthodox Jews outside Israel)	Rosh Hashanah (New Year)
		*10th	Yom Kippur (Day of Atonement)
		*15th-21st	Sukkot (Tabernacles/ Booths)
		*22nd	Simchat Torah (Rejoicing in the Pentateuch)
Heshvan	October-November		
Kislev	November-December	25th – . . .	Chanukkah (Dedication)
Tevet	December-January	. . . – 2nd or 3rd (depending on whether Kislev has 29 or 30 days)	
Shevat	January-February		
Adar	February-March	14th	Purim (Lots)
Nisan	March-April	*15th-*21st (*15th, *16th – *21st, *22nd for Orthodox Jews outside Israel)	Pesach (Passover)
Iyar	April-May	5th (or preceding Thursday if it falls on Friday or Sabbath)	Yom Ha-Atsmaut (Day of Independence)
Sivan	May-June	*6th (*6th- *7th for Orthodox Jews outside Israel)	Shavuot (Pentecost/ Weeks)
Tammuz	June-July		
Av	July-August	9th (or next day if it falls on Sabbath)	Tishah be-Av (9th day of Av)
Elul	August-September		

*Holy Days of rest

3 Main beliefs

The story of how Moses emerged as leader of the Jews is told at the beginning of the biblical book of Exodus. Moses lived in Egypt around 1300 BCE by which time the Jews had been settled there for several hundred years, driven there by famine. They seemed to be such a threat as a thriving immigrant population that they were enslaved and measures were taken to keep down their numbers. When Moses was born into a Jewish family his mother feared for his safety, and when she could no longer hide him she devised a plan. She set him afloat in a basket on the River Nile so that an Egyptian princess would discover him among the bulrushes when she came there to bathe. As planned, the princess took pity on him and adopted him. With his Jewish birthright, but with an Egyptian education and being familiar with court life, Moses was the ideal spokesman for the oppressed Jewish people.

After many years Moses had a deep religious experience in which it is said that God called him from a bush which burned but was not consumed. The Jews believe that this was the same God who had led Abraham, Isaac and Jacob but that he made himself known more fully to Moses by revealing his name and thus his character. Moses used the name 'Yhwh' of God, which seems to come from the Hebrew verb 'to be'. It expresses belief in God's eternal existence: that God is, always has been, and always will be; also that he is the creator, the reason for everything that exists. So holy is the name of God to a Jew that whenever he sees it written down he will say another word meaning 'Lord' instead (Adonai).

In the events that followed, other factors emerged about Moses' God and these have remained basic beliefs in Judaism. Moses was to prove that God was a saviour whose power was made known in historical events. Jews still believe that God is in control of history and that there is a purpose behind everything that happens. Moses was to bring the Jews into a close relationship with God in which they believe that God, although set apart by his holiness, is not totally remote, but concerned for the welfare of mankind. Just as Moses forbade the use of idols, Jews have continued to insist that God is invisible and is so great that no portrayal could ever begin to

Fig. 3   Ashkenazi graves. Notice the Jewish names, the Hebrew writing and the Shield (Star) of David. Sephardi graves are simpler and lie horizontal without headstones. All Jewish graves face towards Jerusalem.

do him justice. There are no Jewish pictures or images of God, even in symbolic form. Moses insisted that they worship God alone. Today Judaism is a passionately monotheistic religion which means that it teaches that there is only one God. This idea is expressed clearly in the opening of the 'Shema', a selection of biblical passages (Deuteronomy 6 verses 4-9, 11 verses 13-21 and Numbers 15 verses 37-41) which are recited daily at morning and evening services:

> Shema Yisrael Adonai Eloheynu Adonai Echad.
> Hear, O Israel: The Lord Our God, The Lord is One.

These are the first words a Jewish child learns, and the last uttered at death. Moses also taught that God was good and required his people to be righteous. Judaism has often been summed up as a religion of ethical monotheism. More will be said about the ethical requirements in chapter 8.

There is no set list of beliefs that Jews must subscribe to; instead the emphasis is much more on Jewish practice. Jews are Jews by virtue of their birth and by identification with the Jewish people; they do not have to experience a moment of personal conversion. Yet a great Spanish Jew of the 12th century, Maimonides, formulated what has come to be accepted as the Thirteen Principles of the Faith. These can be found in the Siddur, the Jewish prayerbook, and express belief that:

1 God is the creator of all
2 God is one
3 God has no body or material form
4 God is eternal
5 God alone is to be worshipped
6 God spoke through the prophets of the Bible
7 Moses was the greatest of all prophets
8 God gave Moses the Law
9 this Law is complete and final
10 God knows everything, even before it happens
11 God will reward the righteous and punish sinners both in this world and the next
12 God will send the Messiah (i.e. a man 'anointed' as leader of the Jews who will be their saviour)
13 God will restore the dead to life

Jews do not recite this as a creed (i.e. statement of belief) but it is clear from the sentiments they express in their worship and the way they live their lives that such beliefs are fundamental to Judaism.

Death and bereavement

It is unlikely that the Jews of Moses' time had much idea of life after death. The traditional Jewish beliefs expressed in articles 11 and 13 above, i.e. in a Day of Resurrection and just rewards in heaven or hell, became fully developed in Judaism after the Hebrew Bible was completed. For all this, the Jewish religion has remained firmly rooted in this world: speculation about what sort of life we shall lead after death has been pushed into the background by the Jewish concern to make *this* world a better place.

Judaism recognises the need to mourn the loss of a loved one and it provides a structure to help the bereaved work through their grief and gradually resume normal life. When a close relative or friend dies, the first week after the burial is one of intense mourning for Jews when they are encouraged to share their feelings with others rather than bottle them up inside. During this time their normal life-style is interrupted and their mourning is symbolised by, for example, sitting on low stools and wearing slippers; men do not shave or have their hair cut, and women do not wear make-up. Orthodox Jews also continue the ancient ritual of rending their garments by making a tear in a lapel: on the left side for parents and on the right side for others; this symbolises the 'tear' that the death has made in their lives. At the end of this period the mourners return to work but maintain a period of semi-mourning until thirty days after the burial. During this time they refrain from celebrations, except Sabbaths. When a parent has died, mourning continues for a full year after burial. During this time Orthodox Judaism requires sons to recite a prayer, called the kaddish, at the three daily synagogue services, and thereafter on the anniversary of the death. This solemn duty brings many who have strayed back into the fold of Judaism. Somewhat surprisingly, the kaddish makes no mention of death but is a prayer which praises God and asks for peace and a good life. It helps the bereaved to accept the death as coming from God and to continue to praise God even in times of sadness. It is also seen as forming a bridge between the living and the dead, who are thought to continue to praise God. The dead are also remembered in prayers on the Day of Atonement, Passover, Pentecost and at the end of Tabernacles. At these times a 24-hour candle is burned for deceased parents as a symbol that the soul is still alive.

Make sure you know
1 the meaning of monotheism
2 whether or not Jews believe in life after death

See if you understand

3 why Jews will not speak the name of God

4 why the Shema is so called

5 the sort of God that Moses believed in

6 how Judaism helps bereaved people to come to terms with their grief

Issues to discuss

7 How can one best cope with a deep sorrow like bereavement: by the 'stiff upper lip' approach or by working through the grief, as Judaism encourages?

8 Take any one of the Thirteen Principles of the Faith and consider its implications as fully as you can.

4 Passover

One of the most important events in the history of the Jews was the exodus. This escape from slavery in Egypt over 3000 years ago is recorded in their Bible, in the book of Exodus (meaning 'exit'). Here we can read of their suffering as their taskmasters tried to break their spirit with heavy labour in the building of great cities; and of the emergence of Moses as their leader. Jews believe that God used Moses as his spokesman to demand from Pharaoh, the ruler of Egypt, the release of the Jews to worship God. Pharaoh's refusal brought one misfortune after another upon Egypt until, after the ninth misfortune, Moses threatened that the last 'plague' would be the death of every first-born child and animal of the Egyptians.

Moses then gave detailed instructions to his own people about how to prepare for their escape. They had to have a good meal inside them and be packed and dressed ready to leave. The blood from the lamb killed for roasting had to be painted on to their door frames as a sign that they were Jews. The story goes on to tell how that night God passed over the houses marked by blood but killed all other first-born in the land of Egypt. When this happened Pharaoh finally agreed to Moses' demands and the Jews left. Then, realising the tremendous loss of slave labour, Pharaoh led his army after them in pursuit. Exodus 14-15 records the miraculous story of how Moses led the Jews safely across the Red Sea (or more likely the Sea of Reeds) as the waters receded, and how the Egyptians were drowned as the waters flowed back again, giving the Jews a safe escape from Egypt.

This momentous escape has been celebrated ever since at Passover, the oldest Jewish festival. It recalls how God *passed over* the Jewish homes marked with blood on the night before the exodus. It is a celebration of freedom, not just from Egypt, but from all oppression ever since, and is a chance for Jews to express the hope that all peoples of the earth will be free. They sometimes refer to it as The Season of our Freedom.

It is also known as The Festival of Unleavened Bread because no yeast is allowed in the home during the entire Passover period and only special unleavened loaves are eaten, called matzot. They look like large, flat, crisp biscuits, either oval or square in shape. This also can be connected with the exodus since the Jews left Egypt in such a hurry that there was no time to leaven their bread with yeast. It also shows that Passover incorporates an ancient harvest festival to give thanks for the barley by offering God pure barley loaves untainted by yeast.

Yet another name for Passover is The Festival of Spring which brings together the previous two titles. Coming at this time of year, the ancient harvest festival of unleavened bread would have been a New Year Festival, symbolised by the deliberate break in the use of the yeast which would normally continue from one bread-making to the next. There is still significance in this today since the week of Passover is a stage-post in the Jewish year, a time for a religious springclean when the Jews break from past sins and make a fresh start. Springtime is also a symbol of freedom since it is a season which bursts free from the cold, dark oppressiveness of winter.

The Passover Festival is celebrated each year for seven days by Jews in Israel and Progressive Jews and for eight days by others, although only the beginning and end of the festival are Holy Days when work is forbidden (see chart on page 9). By far the most important part of it is the Order of Service for the first Night of Passover. So important is this service that it has come to be known simply as the Seder or 'Order'. It says a lot for the importance of family life in Judaism that this service is held in the home, around the meal table, before and after a large supper. It is an occasion when the family gathers together and when grown up children return home and exchange gifts. It is also a time when hospitality is offered to guests, particularly those who would have been alone at Passover.

Careful preparations are made in the home for Passover. The house and especially the kitchen have to be thoroughly cleaned so that all traces of ordinary bread are removed. Most Jews have special Passover sets of crockery, cutlery and cooking utensils that have not come into contact with leaven. Otherwise the existing utensils have to be meticulously cleaned which involves prolonged soaking of china and glass, and metal objects are heated until they glow red hot or scalded in boiling water. On the night before Passover the man of the house makes a ritual search for leaven and his wife will leave one or two crumbs of bread for him to find and ceremoniously sweep up. They are allowed to keep enough bread for breakfast the next morning, but any left over is burned before 11 a.m. along with the crumbs found the previous evening.

The woman of the house is very busy since she goes to great trouble to prepare a special meal for the occasion. She sets the table in a festive fashion with a snowy white cloth and candlesticks. She puts a cushion on the chair to be used by the leader of the Seder and perhaps on everybody's chair. This is a sign that they are no longer slaves like their ancestors in Egypt, but are free to take their time over their meals. She also sets out a wine glass for everyone and makes sure that there are enough bottles for the glasses to be filled four times at certain moments in the service. Several meanings are given to the four cups of wine, the main being the four promises of God in Exodus 6 verses 6-7:

> I will *release* you from your labour in Egypt. I will *rescue* you from slavery there. I will *redeem* you with arm outstretched and with mighty acts of judgement. I will *adopt* you as my people, and I will become your God.

She must also have a special wine cup for Elijah. This is either set in the centre of the table or by a spare place at the table. Jews believe that Elijah, a great biblical prophet, never died and that he will return to usher in the age of peace and goodwill. When the fourth cup of wine is filled, Elijah's cup is also filled in his honour. Some people also leave the door ajar for him or make tapping noises underneath the table to make the children think he is knocking to come in. The wife must also set out symbolic foods such as the unleavened bread itself. Three matzot are covered and placed on top of each other. At the beginning of the Seder the middle one is broken and half is eaten whilst the other half is put aside until the end of the meal. It is customary for it to be hidden and searched for by the children at the end of supper, the finder being rewarded. It is then distributed to be eaten so that its taste lingers on after all else is eaten. Some people keep a little of it for luck, perhaps putting it inside their Seder service book.

There is a service in the synagogue (the place of public worship) to mark the beginning of Passover but usually only the men will have time to attend this. On their return the woman of the house lights the Passover candles, blessing God as she does it, and then the Seder begins. It is essentially the retelling of the exodus story, led by the man of the house who is prompted by four questions put by the youngest child present. The child asks why this night is different from all other nights: why on this night (i) they have unleavened bread (ii) they eat bitter herbs (iii) they dip the herbs and (iv) they recline at table. Each person follows the service in a booklet known as the Haggadah or 'telling'. In this way they all relive again the event of the exodus and come to understand for themselves that God is their saviour who can free them from inner sin and outward oppression. As he retells this long story, draws out its significance and praises God for their deliverance, the leader takes the following symbols which he has before him and uses them as illustrations. (See Fig. 4.)

    1   First he takes a pungent green vegetable such as parsley or celery and dips it into salty water before distributing it for all to eat as an hors d'oeuvre. This has acquired many symbolic meanings: a

Fig. 4 A large family gather for the Seder. The ceremony is being conducted by the man in white who has before him the symbolic foods. Everyone has a Haggadah from which to follow the service. Notice the candlesticks, the wine, and that the men have their heads covered.

green vegetable is a sign of spring and of the rebirth of hope; it also looks like the branches used to paint the doorframes with blood at the exodus; it recalls the meagre diet of the Jews in slavery; and the salt water recalls the tears they shed in Egypt.

2   The next symbol is a roasted bone, traditionally a shankbone of lamb, although sometimes even a neckbone of chicken is used. It is 'roasted' by holding it over the flames of a gas cooker or browning it under an electric grill. It is used to recall the roasted lambs eaten at the exodus, and the lambs sacrificed at Passover when the Temple was still in use.

3   Then the leader takes a whole bitter herb, usually a horseradish, to remind them of the bitter suffering of the Jews in Egypt.

18

4   He dips this into a bowl of charoset and they all eat of it. Charoset is a paste-like mixture of minced apples, walnuts, cinnamon and wine and it symbolises the mortar the slaves used in building the cities for Pharaoh.

5   He may also take some ground bitter herbs or lettuce and make a sandwich of it with the last of the matzot, for all to eat. Just as lettuce tastes sweet at first but leaves a bitter taste in the mouth, so were the Jews at first happy in Egypt and then they suffered bitterly. Sometimes this symbol is replaced by the dish of salt-water.

6   Another symbol is an egg, hard-boiled and then roasted in the same way as the bone. It stands there to represent the fact that burnt offerings were made in the Temple at the three great pilgrim festivals, of which Passover is one. It is also traditional to eat eggs at the first meal after someone is bereaved because it symbolises new life, so here it could represent mourning for the destruction of the Temple where the sacrifices were made. Nothing is done with this roast egg at the Seder but some Jews begin the meal by each eating a hard-boiled egg dipped in salt water.

The main part of the service completed, the family eats dinner together. Then follows the second part of the Seder which consists of prayers, hymns of praise and thanksgiving to God. This looks forward to the future redemption of the Jewish people through the Messianic Age, as a counterbalance to the first part of the Seder which looks back to the redemption of the Jewish people from slavery in Egypt.

Make sure you know
1   which important event is remembered at Passover
2   the three titles given to Passover
3   what matzot are
4   the name of the service on Passover night

See if you understand
5   why a wine goblet is filled for Elijah
6   the significance of each of the four things mentioned by the youngest child (remember the dipping in salt water and charoset)

Further assignments
7   Draw a large seder plate, divided into six sections. In these draw each of the six symbolic foods listed and in a key beneath write down at least one meaning for each.
8   Look again at the explanation of Passover as the Festival of Spring. Take the basic idea of leaving behind the old and looking forward to a new beginning, and consider other symbols of spring like fresh growth and new hope. Now write a poem entitled 'Spring'.

5 A chosen people

Jews believe that Moses was appointed by God and that the exodus was God's saving act on their behalf. They see it as God's choice of Israel as his people, ratified afterwards in a special covenant at Mount Sinai, probably in the southern part of the Sinai Desert. A covenant is an agreement between two parties, freely entered into and binding upon each. The Jews believe that God had previously made a covenant with Abraham, Isaac and Jacob, but that through Moses he entered into a relationship with the whole people:

> Moses came and summoned the elders of the people and set before them all these commands which the Lord had laid upon him. The people all answered together, 'Whatever the Lord has said we will do.' (*Exodus 19 verses 7-8*)

The terms of the Mosaic Covenant were summed up in the Ten Commandments, called the Ten Words, or Decalogue, by Jews:

> The Lord said to Moses, 'Write these words down, because the covenant I make with you and with Israel is in these words.' So Moses . . . wrote down the words of the covenant, the Ten Words, on the tablets. (*Exodus 34 verses 27-28*)

The first four laws are concerned with how God should be worshipped and the rest are about social justice: how God wants his people to treat each other. The Jews believe they were called to remain faithful to God alone and to live in his way. For his part, God promised to bless them and make them prosper as a great nation.

Yet the Mosaic Covenant involved both a promise and a threat:

> Understand that this day I offer you the choice of a blessing and a curse. The blessing will come if you listen to the commandments of the Lord your God which I give you this day, and the curse if you do not listen to the commandments of the Lord your God but turn aside from the way that I command you this day and follow other gods whom you do not know. (*Deuteronomy 11 verses 26-28*)

A priest is set apart as a holy man in his community; he is not necessarily better than others in the sight of God but he is expected to be more religious than the rest and to act as a mediator between God and his people. Similarly the Jews see themselves as having been called out of all the peoples of the earth and as having greater religious demands made upon them. The traditional Jewish blessing, recited on the performance of a commandment, begins:

> Blessed are You, Lord our God, King of the universe, who has made us holy by His commandments and commanded us to . . .

They see their task as 'a light to the nations' (Isaiah 49 verse 6) to lead the rest of mankind to God. They look forward to the Kingdom of God being established, when they will uplift others through their holiness. This hope is here described in poetic terms by the prophet:

> In days to come
> the mountain of the Lord's house
> shall be set over all other mountains
> lifted high above the hills.
> Peoples shall come streaming to it,
> and many nations shall come and say,
> 'Come, let us climb up on to the mountain of the Lord,
> to the house of the God of Jacob,
> that he may teach us his ways
> and we may walk in his paths.'
> For instruction issues from Zion,
> and out of Jerusalem comes the word of the Lord;
> (*Micah 4 verses 1-2*. NB Zion means Jerusalem)

Previously this universalism took the form of active missionary work to convert gentiles to Judaism (such converts are called proselytes); but the militant Christian and Muslim rules virtually stamped this out. A new understanding began to develop within Judaism as it came to accept that theirs was not the only way to God, although it was the only way for them. They believed that people of other religions could also be saved as long as their religion was not idolatrous and taught the natural moral laws demanded by God from the beginning of creation. They recognised that Judaism, with its concept of ethical monotheism, had already inspired the two great world religions of Christianity and Islam. So Judaism became more introspective and concentrated on perfecting itself instead of proselytising. It is only recently, with Progressive Judaism, that there is a growing interest in dialogue with other religions and teaching the world about Judaism. With this trend many of the requirements made of proselytes have been relaxed in Progressive synagogues. In Orthodox synagogues it still involves a long period of study and reflection, sometimes as much as five years; and the conversion must include the traditional ritual of immersion in a special pool, and circumcision beforehand for a man.

Circumcision

Circumcision, the removal of the foreskin, is regarded by Jews as a sign of the covenant, sealed in their flesh. They speak of it as the 'covenant of our father Abraham' since it is associated with this in the biblical account:

> God said to Abraham, 'For your part, you must keep my covenant, you and your descendants after you, generation by generation. This is how you shall keep my covenant between myself and you and your descendants after you: circumcise yourselves, every male among you. You shall circumcise the flesh of your foreskin, and it shall be the sign of the covenant between us.' (*Genesis 17 verses 9-11*)

Circumcision is performed on Jewish boys of eight days old and on male converts to the religion. Most Jewish parents have their sons circumcised even if they are not observant Jews in other respects. Strictly speaking this is not an initiation ceremony and not necessary in order to be recognised as Jewish. On the other hand it is necessary for a convert and even if he is already circumcised he would have to be symbolically recircumcised by the shedding of a drop of blood from his penis. It has always been regarded by the Jew as a supreme sign of loyalty to his religion, as a sign that he must offer his whole self to God, and as a distinguishing mark of the Jew.

The parents invite relatives, friends and neighbours for light refreshments before the ceremony. The circumcision begins with prayers led by the mohel, the one who performs the operation. In the past this used to be the father but it is an experienced circumciser today. The baby boy is brought by his godfather into a room either at home, or in the synagogue, or (in Israel) in a special hall in the hospital. Those present welcome the child and chant biblical verses. The boy is placed for a moment on the special chair set aside for Elijah, since tradition has it that this prophet from the 9th century BCE attends every circumcision. The reason for this tradition is that circumcision is a re-establishment of the covenant between God and the Jews and this is a reminder of the promise of the Messianic Age which, it is thought, Elijah will herald. The baby is then put on the lap of the sandek, someone who has the honoured role of holding him firmly by his legs during the operation. The mohel says a blessing and swiftly snips off the foreskin, tears back the inner lining of the foreskin and stems the flow of blood. Wine is then blessed and, after the naming ceremony, it is drunk and a little is given to the child. The mohel publicly announces the child's Hebrew name for the first time eg 'his name shall be called in Israel David the son of Benjamin'. It is this name which is used in all religious ceremonies even if it is different from that on his birth certificate. Jews believe that they will be called by this name at the Day of Resurrection so that if a baby dies before it is eight days old, it is circumcised at the graveside and given a Hebrew name.

re you know

1   covenant is
2   ewish boys are circumcised
3   circumciser is called

See   **understand**
4 wł   covenant discussed in this chapter can be referred to as
    the   aic or Sinaitic Covenant
5 the meaning of Amos 3 verse 2 (quoted on page 22)
6 what it means to the Jews to regard themselves as God's kingdom
    of priests, his holy nation
7 what circumcision symbolises

Issues to discuss
8 Circumcision is but one of many physical reminders Jews have of
    their religious commitment. Think of some of the different ways
    people generally remind themselves of their religions, from their
    appearance, to their homes and the ceremonies they perform.
    How important do you consider such things to be and would
    religion be better or worse without them?

6 Sabbath

The fourth of the Ten Commandments, recorded in Exodus 20 verses 8-11, begins:

> Remember to keep the sabbath day holy. You have six days to labour and do all your work. But the seventh day is a sabbath of the Lord your God; that day you shall not do any work.

This command is also found in Deuteronomy 5 verses 12-15. Since this is the only festival mentioned in the Ten Commandments, it is the most important of the many Jewish holy days, and many Jews regard it as their most important religious observance.

The Sabbath day is Saturday, the last day of the week, beginning at sunset on Friday evening. Depending on the time of year, this could come at any time between 3 and 8.30 p.m. and Jews must consult a special Jewish calendar for their area or check the time of sunset in their local daily paper. To make it easier, Progressive Jews have set the regular time of 6 p.m. for the Sabbath to start. The Sabbath does not end at sunset on Saturday but at nightfall and therefore lasts approximately 25 hours for an Orthodox Jew (see chapter 2).

The word sabbath means 'to cease' or 'to break off' from ordinary work because it is a day of rest when Jews must put aside all the concerns of their working lives. We have the Jews to thank for the idea of a weekly day of rest, although the Jews themselves regard the Sabbath as their special gift from God and the Sabbath rules as binding upon them alone. Jews are forbidden to work on the Sabbath and down the ages Jewish teachers have tried to define exactly what they can and cannot do at this time. The Talmud (see chapter 7) lists 39 types of forbidden work with numerous subcategories, based on the principle that all creative acts, however small and effortless, count as work. Genesis says that God rested on the seventh day after creating the world, and therefore the Jews rest to commemorate this. It reminds them that it is God's world. In Deuteronomy this commandment is associated with the Jews' escape from Egypt at the exodus, which also makes the point that God is in control and their destiny is in his hands. When Jews cease from any control they may have over the world, they are more likely to remember their utter dependence on God, the all-powerful.

In practice it is still a problem to know what are strictly classed as creative acts and Orthodox Jews take a harder line on this than others. It is generally accepted to cover such things as lighting fires, cooking, carrying, writing, handling money and operating machines. This last category means that Jews cannot drive on the Sabbath or use public transport and they must therefore live close to their synagogues; it forbids using the telephone and even prevents some Jews from switching on electric lights and so forth. Nevertheless modern technology has come to the aid of the Jews with its automatic time switches. Necessary work has always been allowed on the Sabbath, for instance, a doctor would be allowed to practise in an emergency.

All these restrictions do not prevent people enjoying the Sabbath, in fact the reverse is true and mourning is forbidden on this day. The Sabbath gives people a holiday, a period of peace and quiet, of rest and celebration, spent largely at home with their families. There is not the same pace and routine as during the rest of the week and there is plenty of time to worship God and study sacred scriptures. The Sabbath is looked forward to and prepared for like a wedding or a royal visit: Jews speak of it as Israel's 'beloved bride' and 'the Sabbath Queen'. These words are chanted in the synagogue at the Friday evening service:

Come, my friend, to meet the bride;
let us welcome the presence of the Sabbath.

Everyone gets washed and dressed in their best clothes, the housework is done, the best meals of the week prepared, and the table set with the best things. All this preparation is done in advance so that no work is done on the Sabbath. The food often consists of stews which can simmer in the oven on a low heat for as long as necessary.

There are three synagogue services during the Sabbath but often it is only the men who attend the first one on Friday evening since the women are busy at home. This service lasts about 45 minutes and begins shortly after the candlelighting ceremony at home. About 20 minutes before the Sabbath starts the woman of the house, joined by her daughters, lights the Sabbath candles to welcome the Sabbath; light being a symbol of goodness and joy. There must be at least two candles since the Sabbath commandment is recorded twice in the Bible; but sometimes there are as many candles as there are members of the household. The candles must be lit before the Sabbath since this constitutes work. The woman covers her head with a scarf in recognition that God is above her, and lights the candles which are usually set on the meal table in ornate candlesticks. She then covers her eyes with her hands and

Fig. 6 A mother saying the blessing over the Sabbath candles. Notice that the woman's head is covered, that before the girl are the two plaited Sabbath loaves and before the young boy is the wine (can you see which country it comes from?)

28

recites the Hebrew blessing which formally marks the beginning of the Sabbath for her household. Next she says a silent prayer for her home and family which are at the forefront of her mind at this time. The members of the family then greet each other with the words 'Shabbat Shalom' – 'A peaceful Sabbath'.

When the family has all gathered they stand around the meal table and the father places his hand on the head of each of his sons in blessing and says:

> God make you as Ephraim and Menasseh (grandsons of Jacob, a father of the Jewish people).

He does the same to his daughters and says:

> God make you as Sarah, Rebekah, Rachel and Leah (wives of the fathers of the Jewish people).

He follows this by saying:

> The Lord bless you and keep you; the Lord make his face to shine upon you and be gracious unto you; the Lord turn his face unto you and give you peace.

He may then read the passage from Proverbs 31 verses 10-31 on the perfect housewife, in praise of his wife who is not to be taken for granted. Then, lifting a special cup of wine, he pronounces the blessing, or grace, and passes it round the table for everyone to drink. Wine is used since it is traditionally a sign of joy and festivity. Ritual washing of the hands follows at the table, with a blessing. The man then takes the special Sabbath loaves of plaited bread, says a further blessing, breaks or slices it and distributes it for each to eat, dipped in salt. There are always two such loaves at each of the three Sabbath meals, representing the double portion of food collected by the Jews in the Wilderness before the Sabbath day so that they would not have to work on the Sabbath. They can then enjoy the meal, singing Sabbath songs at the end, and often between the courses. A grace is chanted at the end of the meal.

· The next morning the family attends the main service of the week in the synagogue. They return home to eat another meal together which also begins with a blessing over wine. The afternoon is traditionally spent in studying the Scriptures, especially the Talmud, although it is also permitted to sleep, take a leisurely walk, play board games and socialize, which may involve singing and dancing. The last Sabbath meal is a simple one, eaten in the late afternoon before sunset.

The havdalah ceremony

The havdalah ritual follows the Saturday evening service in the synagogue. It is a short ceremony of 'separation' between the holiness of the Sabbath and the week ahead. It may be said at any time after nightfall and is performed both in the synagogue and the home to mark the end of the Sabbath. In the home the family gathers round and the man lights the special havdalah candle. This is made of several thin candles plaited together so that it has more than one wick and so makes sense of the plural form of the prayer which blesses the lights. If a special candle is not available, two candles can be used with their flames held together like a torch. It is forbidden to kindle lights on the Sabbath so it is appropriate that this is the first act of the new week since the Bible says that God created light on the first day of the week. The lighted candle is given to someone else to hold, usually a child, while the man fills the cup with wine and says the blessing over it. He also blesses some fragrant spices, which are usually kept in special, ornate boxes for the purpose. The box of spices is passed round for all to smell, to remind them of the sweetness of the Sabbath during the working week ahead. He says a further blessing, looking at the candle, thanking God for the gifts of light. The cup of wine is then picked up and the ceremony ends with the havdalah prayer being said, which blesses God for the separation of the Sabbath from the rest of the week. The candle is extinguished by dipping the wick in the wine. So ends the Sabbath day and Jews prepare to work hard for another week.

Make sure you know
1 which commandment instructs the Jews to keep the Sabbath
2 when the Sabbath day starts and finishes
3 the meaning of the name 'Sabbath'
4 the meaning of the name 'havdalah'

See if you understand
5 how Jews regard the Sabbath (try to think of at least four key words or phrases)
6 why there are two special loaves at each Sabbath meal

Issues to discuss
7 Jews regard the Sabbath as a foretaste of the coming Kingdom of God. What features of the Sabbath do you think they expect to find when God establishes his perfect kingdom?
8 How does the Sabbath help to keep a Jewish family close together? Are there any lessons to be learned here by others?

Further assignment
9 Imagine you are a strict Orthodox Jew or Jewess and write a full diary entry for a Sabbath Day.

7 Holy Scriptures

Moses is remembered not only for leading the Jews to freedom at the exodus, but also as the one who transmitted to them their most important scriptures. Jews still call him Moshe Rabbenu, 'Moses our Teacher'. The exodus marked the end of a period of slavery, but it was only the beginning of a period of adventure in the Sinai desert under Moses' leadership. This Wilderness Period is said to have lasted 40 years, a round figure representing a generation. During this time it was necessary for Moses to institute laws to govern the people's behaviour. Jews believe that God gave Moses these laws and also helped him to interpret them in specific situations. As will be explained, this constituted both the Torah (the first part of the Hebrew Bible) and the Talmud, which are the most important holy scriptures in Judaism.

The Jewish Bible is known by Christians as the Old Testament, but as the Jews do not accept the claims of Christianity and have no New Testament, they obviously do not recognise this title since it implies that their Bible is outdated and superseded by the Christian New Testament. The Hebrew name the Jews use for their Bible is Tenach. This word is made up from the Hebrew initials of the three sections of their Bible: Torah, Neviim and Ketuvim (Teaching, Prophets and Writings). Its contents were fixed by the end of the 1st century CE.

Virtually all of this Bible was originally written in Hebrew and it is still read in this language today. Many Jewish children are taught Hebrew from an early age in addition to their everyday language, except in the State of Israel where it is the official language. Hebrew is written from right to left, working downwards from the top of the page so that books start at what would normally be the back in an English book. There are only 22 letters in the Hebrew alphabet and these are all consonants. In the 7th century CE a system of dots and dashes above and below the letters was devised to show people what vowel sounds to make so that they could pronounce the words properly. But the biblical scrolls in the synagogues have no such markings, nor are there any punctuation marks or word divisions. Considerable learning is needed to read them fluently and to intone the passages for the readings at the synagogue services.

The **Torah** is the most important of all the Jewish scriptures. Although this word is sometimes used to refer to the entire Hebrew

31

scriptures, in its strictest sense it refers to the first section of the Hebrew Bible, which is also known as the Pentateuch because it consists of 'five books'. These books are commonly known as Genesis, Exodus, Leviticus, Numbers and Deuteronomy, but their Hebrew names are taken from the opening phrase of each book which in English would be: In the beginning, Names, And He called, In the desert and Words. Torah literally means 'teaching' and these books teach about God, people and the world. They open with stories of the creation of the world and early people; then they concentrate on the patriarchs, or forefathers of the Jewish people; and bring the story up to include Moses who led them to the land of Israel.

Most of the Torah is taken up with detailed laws on how to worship God and how to organise society. For this reason Torah is sometimes assumed to mean 'law'. Traditionally the Torah is known as the Five Books of Moses and Orthodox Judaism still maintains that the words of these books were revealed directly to Moses by God on Mount Sinai and that Moses himself wrote them all down perfectly, apart from the last few verses which record his own death. Progressive Judaism is more willing to accept the results of biblical scholarship which suggest that the Torah was compiled over a long period of about 400 years. Yet they still regard it as written by people who were divinely inspired and as the earliest revelation of God's laws to mankind, even though some of these laws may now be outdated. For all Jews the Torah is the source of their religion and is regarded as the most important guide anyone can have in life. The whole of it is read in the course of a year at synagogue services.

The rest of the Hebrew Bible, known as the Prophets and the Writings, does not have the same status as the Torah; although inspired, its words are not thought to have come directly from God and these writings are not as ancient as the Torah. Nevertheless there is a reading from the **Prophets**, at the Sabbath morning services, chosen to match the theme of the Torah reading. The prophets are regarded as the great spokesmen for God and many prophetic passages are outstanding for their literary quality and high ethical demands.

Parts of the **Writings** are used in synagogue services, some at special festivals. This section is considered to be the least sacred of the three and contains material which was largely written later, such as the Book of Daniel which was probably the last, written in the 2nd century BCE. Perhaps its most important book is the collection of 150 psalms, or hymns. These are valued for their deep insights into the relations between God and people and for their beautiful poetry. Some of them are still used regularly in Sabbath worship in the synagogues and many shorter passages are incorporated into

present. Later in the week a reception is given by the boy's parents and the boy makes a speech. This is criticised by some for being too lavish and expensive an affair these days, and for losing its religious significance; but others think a big celebration is justified as the young man enters a new stage in his life.

Girls come of age in Judaism at the age of twelve but since a girl's status in the synagogue changes very little when she becomes a woman, there used to be no public recognition of this. In the early 19th century the Bar Mitzvah was replaced in some German Reform congregations by a confimation service for both boys and girls, often when they were in their late teens, following a course of instruction in Judaism. This ceremony is still found among some Progressive Jews and it usually occurs at the feast of Pentecost (Shavuot). It has led to a greater recognition of girls in Judaism and some synagogues, even some Orthodox ones, have now introduced an equivalent to a boy's Bar Mitzvah, known as the Bat Mitzvah ('daughter of the commandment'). There is no fixed procedure for this ceremony yet, although it is usually held for a group of girls at a time.

The Day of Atonement

Jews recognise that, however hard they try to live up to the perfect law of God, everyone falls short of it and so there is built into the Jewish system the means of forgiveness. Jews believe that God is loving and merciful to those who truly repent and although forgiveness can be sought at any time, there is a special fast associated with it called Yom Kippur, the Day of Atonement.

This comes soon after Rosh Hashanah, the New Year festival, a particularly appropriate time for taking stock of one's life over the past year and making a fresh start. Rosh Hashanah is a joyful celebration when sour or pickled foods are avoided and instead sweet things are eaten, like pieces of apple dipped in honey, to symbolise the 'sweetness' of rejoicing. Nevertheless, the blasts of the ram's horn (called a shofar), blown in synagogue at the special morning service on this day, have been interpreted as a call to the conscience.

The next ten days are solemn days in which Jews try to remember all the things they have done wrong. They believe that sin against God, such as failure to keep the Sabbath, can be forgiven by God; but where they have wronged another person they have to do all they can to get themselves out of this situation by asking his forgiveness and making amends. So this is a period of deep heart-searching, of honesty with oneself and humility. It forces people to bring out into the open anything which may have hurt another person and which has not been properly resolved. It encourages people to put right any bad feelings between them, to seek and to grant forgiveness. Only when this is done are Jews worthy to ask

God's forgiveness for the sins they cannot put right themselves. So they hope for salvation and pray that their names will be inscribed in the Book of Life for another year.

Yom Kippur is a day of fasting as a sign of being sorry for one's sins. From sunset to nightfall the next day it is forbidden to eat, drink or have sex, and only the hands and face may be washed. These rules do not apply to the sick and elderly nor to those who become faint whilst fasting. Nor do they apply to girls under 12 and boys under 13, although children over nine may fast for a short time to get into training for when they are old enough.

So important is Yom Kippur that most of the day is taken up with five long synagogue services. The first, which takes place in the evening, is called Kol Nidre and is one of the most important services of the year. Consequently it is always well attended. At each service everyone joins in a prayer of confession which covers almost every possible aspect of sin. The fact that the plural 'we' is used shows the communal feeling within Judaism and recognition of collective responsibility. Sin is not regarded as a private matter, it is a wrong which taints the whole community. Similarly it is often the society we live in which tempts us to sin and there is therefore a sense of shared guilt.

Yom Kippur ends with a single blast of the shofar and afterwards there is eating and rejoicing in the assurance that sins are forgiven and the burden of guilt removed.

Make sure you know
1 where you would expect to find a mezuzah
2 what is a tallit
3 the usual age at which a Jewish boy is made bar mitzvah
4 the name of the equivalent ceremony for girls

See if you understand
5 why it is possible to describe even the social laws of Judaism as religious laws
6 why Jews are thankful for the commandments
7 what Judaism requires of people who claim to be sorry for wronging others

Issues to discuss
8 Consider if Hillel's 'golden rule' is a good enough guide to every moral dilemma. Can you improve on it?
9 Do you agree with the Jewish idea of collective responsibility for the sins committed by individuals in a society? Can you think of examples to support this idea?

9 Food

Many of the Jewish laws make sense when we understand their origins amongst a nomadic, desert people. Judaism encompasses every area of life, nothing being considered too humdrum to fall outside God's concerns; there is even a traditional blessing to be said on going to the toilet in the morning. It would be impossible to even mention most of the commandments here, let alone to investigate them properly, so rather than attempt this we shall just look at one aspect of Jewish daily life in some detail. However little people know about Judaism, most seem to know that Jews don't eat pork. So we shall consider the Jewish dietary rules and you will see that abstention from pork is just a tiny part of the whole. The Jewish concern for accuracy in following God's teaching in even the smallest details is evident here, for there is a deep desire to uphold God's standards which he has made known to his people for their benefit. Some of these rules were obviously important in the Wilderness for hygienic reasons but now, even with modern refrigeration to keep meat fresh, the rules still apply. Jews continue to follow them not primarily for health reasons but to fulfil God's commandments by which he has set them apart as a holy people. It must be said, however, that Progressive Jews are less concerned to keep all the food laws for the very reason that they do see them as outdated, and thus consider them to be man-made rules rather than God's unchanging commands.

All Jewish food must be 'kosher' which means it is 'fit' for use in accordance with Jewish law, sometimes described as 'clean'. Vegetables and cereal products easily pass the test as long as they are washed clean of insects. Other foods have to fulfil far more requirements, especially meat. First, only certain animals are permitted to be eaten. These are listed in Leviticus 11 and Deuteronomy 14. The permitted animals are those which both chew the cud and have a parted foot or cloven hoof. This includes cattle, sheep, goats and deer but not animals like rodents, which are considered unclean. They have to fulfil both requirements so that pigs are rejected because they do not chew the cud, and camels and horses because they do not have cloven hooves. Poultry is acceptable: chickens, capons, turkeys, ducks and geese, but not birds of prey or carrion (eaters of dead meat, e.g. vultures). The eggs of permitted birds can be eaten unless they have a spot of blood in them in which case they must be thrown away. The importance of the blood is discussed in the next paragraph. Fish are permitted as long as they are a variety which has both fins and scales, but other sea and fresh water creatures are forbidden, like crabs, shellfish, eels and frogs.

Meat must not be eaten from animals which have died naturally, but every animal and bird must be ritually slaughtered with a blessing. It is done by a highly skilled Jew who slits its throat as painlessly as possible with one stroke of a sharp knife. The blood which gushes out is drained away and not eaten in the meat. This is because the blood represents to the Jew the life of the animal and all life is recognised as given by God. There was an ancient custom of collecting the life-blood in a bowl and splashing it against the altar by way of offering the life back to God. The animal is then inspected to make sure there are no traces of disease.

Certain parts of the animal are forbidden: the hard fat below the diaphragm known as the suet, and the sciatic nerve. The fat is forbidden since it was originally used for burning on the altar. The sciatic nerve in the thigh is forbidden in memory of the biblical story in which it is said that Jacob wrestled all night with God and

> . . . he struck him in the hollow of his thigh, so that Jacob's hip was dislocated as they wrestled. (*Genesis 32 verse 25*)

Since it is difficult to extract the sciatic nerve or even the major arteries, quite often the whole hindquarters of the animal are discarded.

Next the meat must be thoroughly washed to remove any further traces of blood. This involves soaking in water for about half an hour to open up the pores and then the meat is sprinkled with salt and left so it absorbs the blood for an hour, and finally rinsed again. All meat is well cooked to remove any final traces of blood and this is especially important with liver which cannot be drained of its blood by soaking and salting.

A final prohibition is that it is forbidden to cook and eat milk and meat together (this includes poultry but not fish). This stems from a law found three times in the Torah:

> You shall not boil a kid in its mother's milk. (*Exodus 23 verse 19, 34 verse 26, Deuteronomy 14 verse 21*)

This seems to reflect a particular pagan practice, but it has led the Jews to separate completely meat and milk and their products. They use separate cooking utensils and crockery and never mix the two types of food or serve them at the same meal. After eating meat, a time limit of usually not less than three hours is maintained before anything milky can be eaten. However, meat can be eaten quite soon after milk products (except for hard cheese), as long as the mouth and hands are cleaned between the two: the mouth should be washed out and a hard substance like bread chewed to remove the taste of the milk. There is no great time lapse this way round because the mouth can be cleansed more easily of milk products than of meat whose particles may cling to the teeth. The Jew must make sure that pastry made with milk is not used with meat or that pastries which contain milk are not cooked in animal fat. All these rules are there to prevent the milk and meat being eaten together.

The Jewish food laws, if observed, affect a Jew every day of his life, reminding him constantly that he is called by God to be holy in all that he does. Such rules have obviously set the Jew apart from his gentile neighbour since a Jew must buy his food in kosher food shops, especially butchers, where he can be sure that it fulfils the Jewish requirements. Equally, a strict Jew will not eat food cooked by a gentile and therefore he can only eat out in Jewish restaurants. Jewish food has therefore been an important ingredient in maintaining Judaism through the ages, and many a Jewish family is held together today by its gatherings around the meal table and its sharing in the traditional Jewish foods, even if other Jewish rules are overlooked.

Tabernacles

Each festival has its own traditional foods and this is especially evident at Sukkot, or 'Tabernacles', since it was originally an autumn harvest thanksgiving and still retains many features of this. The tabernacles, or booths, were makeshift huts constructed in the fields at the end of the grape and olive harvest. The whole family stayed there for the ingathering of the fruits, living on the job and keeping watch over their produce. When all was safely gathered in there were great celebrations.

This festival was given a further religious meaning when the huts were associated with the tents that the Hebrews lived in during the Wilderness Period. So it is a reminder for Jews of this early formative period, the flimsy huts being symbolic of their utter dependence on God and willingness to move at his bidding.

Today huts are still constructed to celebrate this festival even though most Jews no longer belong to agricultural communities. It is a way of reliving the past experiences of their people and to feel again this dependency on God for food and shelter, as well as to pray that God will continue to 'tabernacle' or live among them. The hut, called a sukkah (singular of sukkot), should be between one and ten metres high and should have a roof made of branches through

Fig. 9   A sukkah on a kibbutz in Israel. During the week of the Feast of Tabernacles this large sukkah replaces the usual communal dining room. It is constructed of branches, through which the light shines. You will notice because of the grass underfoot that it is out of doors.

which you can see the sky. It is furnished inside so that the family can at least eat their meals there even if the climate prevents them from living and sleeping there. It is decorated with greenery, flowers, fruit and vegetables as a reminder of its harvest character. Some Jewish families build their own hut in the garden, often as a lean-to against the house. This is often difficult with modern housing, particularly flats, and it is interesting to see that in Israel flats are being designed so that they have at least one balcony which is not beneath another but open to the sky, on which a sukkah can be properly constructed. Where it is not practicable to build a real one, a symbolic one can be constructed of trellis work put up on a window ledge and decorated with fruit and foliage. Or a sliding roof might be incorporated in one of the rooms of the synagogue to be opened to the sky during Tabernacles, so that the room symbolises a sukkah.

The first day of Tabernacles is a holy day of rest when Jews celebrate together. The best meal is eaten on the first evening and traditionally this consists of stuffed cabbage or vine leaves, followed by fresh fruits, especially those grown in Israel, like oranges, dates and figs.

Apart from the sukkah, the other traditional symbols are four plants: the citron, palm, myrtle and willow. This is in fulfilment of the biblical commandment:

> On the first day you shall take the fruit of citrus-trees, palm fronds, and leafy branches, and willows from the riverside, and you shall rejoice before the Lord your God for seven days. (*Leviticus 23 verse 40*)

The three branches are bound together and held in the right hand and the citrus fruit in the left hand with its stem downwards. The two hands are then held close together and waved in the four directions of the compass as well as up and down. This symbolises God's sovereignty over all and is repeated whenever they go into the sukkah. It is also done at all synagogue services during the festival when the joyful Hallel (Psalms 113-118) is recited.

The Rabbis said these four plants symbolise the four different types of people, all of whom are bound up with each other in life so that we are all responsible for each other. The citron is best for it has both taste and fragrance and represents those who have learning of God's commandments and also carry them out. The palm produces tasty dates but has no fragrance and so it represents those who have learning but not good deeds. The myrtle, with its fragrance but no taste, is like those with good deeds but no learning, while the willow has neither.

Tabernacles is a time of great rejoicing, of giving and receiving of presents within the family and of taking baskets of fruit to the sick and housebound.

Make sure you know
1 what 'kosher' means
2 how animals must be killed if the meat is to be eaten by Jews
3 what type of food Jews must not eat with meat
4 what a sukkah looks like

See if you understand
5 why Jews soak and salt their meat and also cook it thoroughly
6 why the Festival of Tabernacles commemorates the Wilderness Period

Further assignments
7 Using Leviticus 11 verses 1-30 and Deuteronomy 14 verses 3-20, make two columns, listing the forbidden and permitted animals, sea creatures, birds and insects.
8 Read carefully through the Jewish food laws, noting any which are important for health as well as for religious reasons (for example, meat from animals found dead, which is forbidden, might be diseased or decayed).
9 Plan a menu for a three-course meal which an Orthodox Jew would be permitted to eat.

10 The Temple

Whilst Moses was leader, the Jews were constantly on the move, pressing onwards towards the Promised Land. They lived as nomads, like the Arab Bedouins who still inhabit these desert regions and travel with their animals from one water hole to another, always seeking new pastures in order to stay alive. Under such conditions the only religious shrine the Hebrews could have was a portable one, kept in a sturdy tent. It was built to Moses' instructions after he had returned from Mount Sinai and was known as the Tent of Meeting because here God was believed to meet and speak with his people. The most important part of the shrine was the Ark of the Covenant, a small wooden chest in which were kept the two stone tablets inscribed with the Ten Commandments. The Ark could be carried from place to place by inserting long poles into rings at the bottom in each corner.

It was not until King David established Jerusalem as his capital city that the Ark arrived at its final resting place. Under David the shrine continued to be a tent, or 'tabernacle', but in the reign of his son Solomon in the 10th century BCE an impressive temple was built in Jerusalem. Within the temple building was an inner shrine, the 'holy of holies', which contained the Ark. This temple stood until 586 BCE when it was destroyed by enemy action and the Exile followed. No more was heard of the Ark. When the exiles returned towards the end of that century they rebuilt the temple, referred to as the Second Temple. They needed a place for their priests to offer sacrifices to God in order to make amends for their sins, and where Jews could worship at least three times a year at the great pilgrim festivals.

The Temple remained the centre of Judaism and in the 2nd century BCE it became the rallying point for a nationalist revolt against their foreign overlords who were trying to impose pagan culture. This came to a head under the Seleucid ruler of Syria, Antiochus IV who was called Epiphanes because he regarded himself as a 'manifestation' of the god Zeus. He forbade the Jews to study or follow the Torah and made them offer sacrifices to Zeus on pain of death. In 167 BCE he desecrated the Temple by setting up an altar to Zeus over the original altar and sacrificing pigs on it, which are 'unclean'

49

animals to Jews. This high-handed action was enough to spark off the rebellion that had been smouldering. It was led by the priestly Hasmonean family, one of whom was Judas and whose nickname 'Maccabee' (Hebrew for 'hammer') gave its name to the Maccabean Revolt. So zealously did they fight to defend Judaism that they defeated Antiochus' army and demanded a peace treaty. One of the first things Judas did was to cleanse the Temple of its foreign pollution by rebuilding a new altar on the same model as the previous one and renewing all the furnishings and sacred implements. It was rededicated exactly three years after its desecration. The quarrel with the Seleucids continued for another twenty-five years until finally independence was won and the Hasmonean Dynasty was established which lasted for nearly a century.

Chanukkah

This story of the survival of Judaism and freedom from oppression is celebrated each year at the festival of Chanukkah, which means 'dedication'. It is told in the apocryphal books of I and II Maccabees, books which are not included in the Hebrew Bible but which are considered to be of historical interest. There we are told:

> There was great merry-making among the people, and the disgrace brought on them by the Gentiles was removed.
> Then Judas, his brothers, and the whole congregation of Israel decreed that the rededication of the altar should be observed with joy and gladness at the same season each year, for eight days, beginning on the twenty-fifth of Kislev. (*I Maccabees 4 verses 58-59*)

This festival is still kept alive by Jews today and, although it is only a minor festival because it is not mentioned in the Pentateuch, it has become particularly important for Jews in Christian countries because it has many similarities with Christmas which is also a mid-winter festival of light. Jews still celebrate Chanukkah for eight days; the reason for this is explained in the Talmud. There the legend is recorded that when the great seven-branched candelabrum ('menorah' in Hebrew) of the Temple was lit there was found to be only enough olive oil to burn for one day, and yet miraculously it lasted for eight. This is commemorated by lighting eight candles at Chanukkah and it is known as the Festival of Lights. Jews have special candlesticks for the occasion called Chanukiyot (plural of Chanukkiyah). They have eight or nine branches, the ninth being for the 'servant' candle which is used to light the others. One candle is lit on the first night, then two on the second night, and so on until all eight are lit by the last day. The candles are lit after dark, immediately after the stars appear, and must burn for at least half an hour. The candlesticks are placed by a window so that the light

the Jewish martyrs. Many Jews fast throughout the whole day or at least avoid lavish foods and festivities as a sign of sadness. In the synagogues the curtain is removed from before the Ark and the lights dimmed. Worshippers gather there, to sit on the ground or on low stools as a sign of mourning, and chant the Lamentations of the Prophet Jeremiah, and other special poems are read which refer to various tragedies in Jewish history. Jews still feel such a sense of continuity with their past that they weep genuine tears for the sorrows of bygone ages.

Make sure you know
1 where the Jewish Temple was built
2 what remains of it today
3 what three things have taken over from the offering of sacrifices in Judaism

See if you understand
4 why the Jews still celebrate the rededication of the Temple which took place over 2000 years ago
5 why Jews still mourn the destruction of the Temple

Issues to discuss
6 Why do you think most Jews want to visit the remains of the Temple, and Israeli Jews perform many religious ceremonies there? How important is it for a religion to have places of pilgrimage?

11 Worship

Since the destruction of the Second Temple, the main places for Jewish public worship have been the synagogues. There is considerable debate over when synagogues first started. It seems likely that they did not develop until the 2nd century BCE in the form of 'meeting places', as we know them today. Nevertheless local 'gatherings' for worship (the original meaning of the Greek word 'synagogue') would presumably have occurred much earlier and would have been particularly important during the Exile when the Jews needed to meet together to sustain their faith.

With the destruction of the Temple, the priesthood ceased to function and the religious leaders associated with the synagogues, the rabbis, became the leaders of Judaism. They were not seen as mediators between God and man as the priests had been, but as 'teachers' of Judaism, which is what their name means. Their traditional role in synagogue worship was to preach the sermon, but they often take a greater part in leading the services today. The running of the synagogue is done by elected elders who can be recognised by the top hats they often wear in synagogue.

Today synagogues have many architectural forms, depending on the time and place in which they are built. Sometimes rich Jewish communities construct lavish synagogues but quite often they are very ordinary buildings. Synagogues were never intended to rival or replace the Temple and therefore they are often intentionally nondescript. There are seven main Jewish symbols used to decorate them: the Shield (or Star) of David (see Fig. 13); the Olive Branch; the Pomegranate; the Vine Clusters; the Seven-branched Candlestick, reminiscent of the menorah of the First Temple; the Star of Solomon; and the Lion of Judah. In view of the second commandment, no image of God is permitted, and there is even a reticence to portray the human form or other pictorial or sculptural representations because of the strict prohibition of idolatry. The most important thing about a synagogue is that it should be serviceable since it is used not only as a place of divine worship but also as a community centre with meeting rooms and reception areas, and as a place for Jewish teaching and studies. The synagogue is therefore a House of Prayer, a House of Study and a House of Assembly.

The most important part of a synagogue is the sanctuary where the congregation gather for worship. In Orthodox synagogues men and women are strictly segregated so there would be a balcony for the women or a screen to separate them from the men, just as they were separated into the men's and women's courtyards in the Temple. Progressive Jews have accepted the modern attitude of the greater equality of men and women so that both sexes can mix freely in their synagogues and women can take a public part in the services. There are even some women rabbis.

The focal points of the sanctuary are the Holy Ark and the reading desk. The Ark is a special cupboard, often built into the eastern wall, in which is kept one or more scrolls containing the Torah. These scrolls are meticulously handwritten in Hebrew by Jewish scribes with a goose quill pen on sheepskin parchment which is then attached to wooden rollers at each end. It takes between a year and eighteen months to complete such a scroll and they are so precious that they are wrapped in ornate velvet covers and decorated with silver ornaments. The Torah scrolls are kept in the Ark which is usually closed and has a beautifully embroidered curtain drawn across the doors. Above it, from the ceiling, hangs the Perpetual Light which is always alight. The cupboard is called the Ark after the Mosaic Ark of the Covenant in which were kept the Ten Commandments. The curtain represents the curtain which sealed off the Holy of Holies in which the Ark was kept in the Temple. Similarly there was a lamp kept burning in the Temple, symbolising the presence of God; it is also a sign of respect for the holiness of the Torah Scrolls and is a symbol of the enlightenment which comes from knowledge of the Torah. On the wall above the Ark there is often a representation of the two stone tablets of the Ten Commandments, usually with only the first two Hebrew words of each commandment on it. Or an appropriate text may be inscribed here in Hebrew, either from the Bible or the Talmud, such as 'Know before whom you stand' (Talmud). The scrolls are read at the reading desk from which most of the rest of the service is also conducted. This desk, known as the bimah, is on a raised platform and is traditionally placed in the centre of the sanctuary, with the reader facing the Ark in the East wall, in the direction of Jerusalem, and with the congregation's seats facing inwards. However, Progressive synagogues now frequently have the reading desk along with the pulpit at the front of the sanctuary, facing the congregation.

Jews should pray from their prayer books three times a day: in the morning, afternoon and evening. There are extra prayers at festivals and at special times like bereavement. The daily prayers may be said privately but there is a strong sense of community amongst Jews and they tend to gather together for the daily services, although this need not be in a synagogue if somewhere else is

Fig. 11   The interior of an Orthodox synagogue during a service. The Holy Ark is open for a scroll to be removed. It will be carried in solemn procession to the bimah in the centre of the synagogue (bottom left of the picture). Notice the women's gallery. What other Jewish features can you spot in this picture?

more convenient, like at work or at home. A service can take place as long as there are at least ten Jewish men present (known as a minyan). Some Progressive synagogues recognise a minyan of both men and women, but the traditional emphasis on men accepts that women may be preoccupied in the home and therefore are not obliged to attend the services.

The main service in the synagogue is the Sabbath one held on Saturday morning. This lasts for about three hours in Orthodox synagogues and about half this time in Progressive synagogues. Apart from the sermon, the service is almost entirely in Hebrew in Orthodox synagogues but most of the prayer-books contain translations. There is far less Hebrew used in Progressive synagogues but some is retained as a bond between Jews all over the world. Some Progressive synagogues have introduced musical instruments, such as organs, but traditionally the Jews have not had such music since the destruction of the Temple, as a sign of mourning. Nevertheless, a form of music plays an important part in synagogue worship since all the prayers and Bible readings, including the Psalms, are chanted in special traditional ways, reflecting their mood. There is often a highly-trained cantor to lead the prayers who must have a fine voice and musical ability.

Jews wash their hands before prayer and dress respectfully for worship: Orthodox Jewish women cover their heads with scarves and the men wear hats or skull-caps. The men also wrap a prayer-shawl (called tallit) round their shoulders to symbolise communion with God and to remind them of the commandments (see page 39). The tallit is worn at all morning services. The worshippers stand for prayer, which is also a sign of respect.

The Sabbath service consists of prayers and Bible readings, with most sections preceded and followed by benedictions, or prayers 'blessing' God. The most important prayer is simply called the Tefillah, or 'prayer', and at least part of it is included in all statutory services. It is also known as the Amidah, meaning 'standing' because it is said in this position. It has 19 sections which praise God, ask him to satisfy both spiritual and physical needs of the individual and the community, and thank him for all his goodness. This prayer is first said in silence by the worshippers and then repeated by the cantor with the congregation joining in the responses.

The central part of the service is the reading of the Torah. The Ark is opened to display the Torah scrolls, each of which contains all five books of the Torah. One is removed and carried in solemn procession around the sanctuary to the reading desk. The covering of the Torah scroll is often decorated with little bells so that a sweet sound accompanies its movement. Members of the congregation touch the scroll as it passes, often with the tallit fringes which they then kiss. There is a set portion from the Torah for each Sabbath, to be read in all synagogues. It is subdivided into seven sections which are usually read by different men present. They must not run their fingers over the precious scroll itself and so they keep their place with a pointer as they chant the Hebrew from right to left. It is considered an honour to be called up for this and people are often chosen if it is a special time for them such as a boy's bar mitzvah (see chapter 8), a bereavement or a forthcoming marriage. If the person is not able to read the Hebrew passage he will just recite the blessing at the beginning and end of the section and leave the more difficult part to the cantor. Afterwards the Torah scroll is returned and a reading follows on a similar theme from a book which contains selected passages from the Prophets. Then follows a sermon and the service ends with more prayers.

After the Sabbath service they return home. It is the home which is essential for Jewish worship: the place where the whole family gathers around the meal table to share their Jewish faith day by day. At the table, ancient traditions are perpetuated: candles are lit, prayers are said, their history is relived and religious songs are sung. Before and after a meal lengthy thanksgivings are recited. The home is the centre of Jewish life and worship, where Judaism is absorbed along with the tastes and smells and where worship comes naturally. There is no distinction in Judaism between everyday and religious things; they find God in every part of life and constantly find reasons for blessing him.

All Jewish services, whether at home or in the synagogue, are taken from a prayer book, called the Siddur ('order' or 'arrangement'), which has grown up over the ages. Progressive synagogues use different prayer books to the more traditional authorised version, but the prayers are all founded on biblical texts, especially from the Psalms. They may not sound like prayers, in the sense of asking God for something, but they are often expressions of hope and trust in God. Therefore much Hebrew prayer is repetitious, but this is valued since it is in repeating familiar words that new meanings can be seen in them. The Hebrew word for prayer means 'to judge oneself' showing that the aim is for Jews to change themselves through prayer rather than just expecting God to change their situation for them. It involves their looking deep into themselves and measuring what they see against the high demands of their religion and against the perfection of God.

58

Make sure you know

1 what the name 'synagogue' means
2 the three main purposes for which a synagogue is used
3 one of the names of the most frequently used Jewish prayer
4 how many daily services there are in the Jewish prayer book

See if you understand

5 why there are no images of God in the synagogues
6 why the Ark is the focal point of the synagogue
7 why some Jews find it difficult to do the Torah reading in the service

Issues to discuss

8 Why do you think synagogues became so popular in Judaism, setting the pattern for congregational worship in Christianity also? Consider particularly the appeal they might have held for ordinary people, over Temple worship.
9 Consider fully how prayer can be a means of 'judging oneself'.

Further assignment

10 From the information and photograph in this chapter, draw a plan of an Orthodox synagogue and another of a Progressive synagogue and label them fully.

12 Anti-Semitism

Anti-Semitism, that is prejudice against Jews, has existed for almost as long as the Jews themselves. They knew slavery in Egypt 3000 years ago and have suffered intermittently ever since. Some of the worst atrocities against Jews have been committed in the 20th century and anti-Semitism is still found in some areas today.

The reasons for this are varied and complex but a basic reason is that the Jews have mostly lived in foreign countries and minority immigrant populations are easy scapegoats for the problems of society. Also, during the Middle Ages, Jews were forced to live together in separate quarters. These became known as 'ghettoes' after one such settlement in 16th century Venice which was situated near a foundry ('getto' in Italian). The ghettoes were usually surrounded by high walls and the gates were locked at night. This segregation caused the rest of the people to regard the Jews as different from themselves, and to be suspicious and frightened of them. In turn it increased the Jews' sense of identity with fellow Jews, it made them inward-looking and less willing to mix with non-Jews and it strengthened their religion and spirit of resistance.

One of the worst persecutions of the Jews took place under Hitler's Nazi regime of Germany during the Second World War. Hitler considered the Jews to be an 'inferior race', even sub-human, and he did all he could to separate them from normal German life and to poison the minds of others against them, especially the German youth. In 1942 the 'final solution' was devised to purge Europe of all its Jews. In Germany and Nazi-occupied countries of Europe the Jews were rounded up and packed off to concentration camps. Many Jews resisted bravely in the ghettoes, but the conditions in the camps were so appalling and dehumanising that even the will to live was soon quenched. Men, women and children were herded together like animals and taken by rail in overcrowded trucks to any of the twenty-eight camps, whose names like Dachau, Buchenwald and Bergen Belsen have since become infamous. There the strongest were used in slave labour and the weakest simply murdered. Countless women and children died in gas chambers. The worst death camps were in Poland, such as Auschwitz in western Poland and Treblinka, 60 miles from Warsaw. Of the 3 million Jews in Poland, only 30 000 (1 in every 100) survived. Of the 15 000 children under 15 years who were taken to the camp in Terezin, Czechoslovakia, only about 100 came back. Of the 16 million Jews in the world at the time, 6 million died in what has become known as the Holocaust.

The results of the Holocaust are still with us today. All the great centres of Jewish life and culture in Eastern and Central Europe were wiped out. Most European Jews can name at least one member of their family who perished in it and some lost all of their close relatives. Those who were liberated from a Nazi prison camp at the end of the war have its tormenting images seared into their memories, just as their serial numbers are still tattooed on their forearms. After the war they may have worked hard to start a new life and a new family but many break down during retirement, when there is time to reflect and the horror returns. Many, scarred by their experiences, are bitter towards and suspicious of gentiles.

Not surprisingly, the Jews are obsessed with the memory of the Holocaust. Time has passed and there is a danger that their own young and the rest of the world will forget the past. They are determined to keep alive its memory as a dreadful warning against the dangers of prejudice, whoever the victim is, and to prevent its repetition. Some of the death-camps remain as silent witnesses of people's inhumanity to each other, and a modern Holocaust Museum has been built in Jerusalem which documents the dreadful history of that time. Its Hall of Remembrance is a holy place that one enters in reverence, keeping quiet and putting on a skull-cap if you are a man. In the dimness burns a perpetual flame in memory of the dead. It lights up the memorial for each of the camps, bearing its name and the number of Jews killed there. At Dachau in southern Germany, now a museum, there is this inscription on the wall:

PLUS JAMAIS
NEVER AGAIN
NIE WIEDER
NIKOGDA BOLSHE

The Holocaust also gave an impetus to the Jewish demand for a homeland and was one of the factors in the United Nations' support for the State of Israel which was established after the war. From the beginning Israel has been a haven for Jews fleeing from persecution. It has recently taken in tens of thousands of Jews from Russia after a long struggle to obtain exit permits. The 3 million Russian Jews have suffered many restrictions under Communism where anti-religious laws prevent children under 18 from attending religious meetings and where religious publications and places of worship are severely limited. Jews everywhere feel that the exist-

Fig. 12   The execution of a Polish Jew by a German officer in the Second World War. Dead bodies lie below him in the grave.

ence of Israel gives them a greater sense of security and, having gained their own country, they have demonstrated a determination to hold on to it against all odds.

Finally, the Holocaust posed for the Jews the disturbing question of why God allows suffering. Judaism has no simple answer to this and I can only hint at some of their lines of thought here. One of the main answers to be found in the Bible is that suffering is sent by God as a punishment for sin, not necessarily of the individual but of society as a whole. There is in Judaism a strong sense of corporate responsibility so that even when individuals are immediately responsible for some crime it is also recognised that they are a product of the society which nurtured them. Many Jews still think that suffering may be deserved: perhaps God's commandments are not being fully and properly observed; or perhaps they have observed them outwardly but not let their meaning really penetrate their hearts. Yet no one could imagine that the Jews really deserved the Holocaust. The blame must lie with the persecutors and not with the victims.

Another traditional Jewish view is that the suffering of the righteous heralds the end of the world and God's ultimate victory. It has been prophesied that the most terrible disasters would come first and that mankind can only be made perfect in the age to come. Yet this does not mean that the Jews have welcomed or passively accepted suffering. They have always been encouraged to work for the coming of that New World here and now by opposing evil and upholding justice and righteousness.

It is understandable if some Jews have lost faith in God in the face of such persecution; but others have taken their religion more seriously. With so many of their leaders and teachers lost, many post-war Jews feel a particular responsibility to keep alive the religion for which their parents died. Some have continued to believe, even in the face of suffering, as these words scratched on a cellar wall in Cologne testify:

I believe in the sun even when it is not shining.
I believe in love even when not feeling it.
I believe in God even when he is silent. (*by an anonymous 20th-century Jew*)

Purim

Purim is a festival which reminds the Jews of their persecution and celebrates their deliverance from annihilation. The incident they recall is told in the biblical book of Esther, a romantic story set during a period about 2400 years ago when Palestine was part of the Persian empire. The story tells how the beautiful, young Esther pleased the King and became his queen, without him knowing her

Jewish origins. Her cousin and guardian, Mordecai, also won favour with the king but he offended Haman, the Prime Minister, because he refused to bow down to him. Mordecai declared that he was a Jew and would worship no one but God. Haman was so angry that he plotted to exterminate all the Jews in that vast empire. The name 'Purim' comes from the fact that he cast 'lots' to fix the date on which he would destroy them. So he laid his plans, initially with the King's consent. Mordecai got word to Esther and asked her to plead with the King for them, even though it was forbidden for anyone to go to the King unbidden. She asked all the Jews to join her in a three-day fast before she did it. Fortunately the King listened to her and when he heard of Haman's wickedness he had him hanged on the gallows that he had prepared for Mordecai. The King gave permission for the Jews to defend themselves against their enemies. This new writ was issued throughout the empire and 'there was joy and gladness for the Jews, feasting and holiday' (Esther 8 verse 17), and so the feast of Purim was inaugurated.

Jews fast on 13th Adar, the day known as the Fast of Esther, but Purim itself is a very jolly occasion. It is celebrated on 14th Adar, the day when Haman's plot was foiled, but a day later in ancient walled cities like Jerusalem since the Jews of Shushan, the walled capital of Persia, were delivered a day later. Consequently the 15th Adar is called Shushan Purim. Purim is not a holy day on which work is forbidden, but since it is such a popular festival it is usually taken as a holiday. People are expected to hear the reading of the book of Esther, preferably in the synagogue from a hand-written scroll of Esther known as the Megillah. It is followed by a blessing which sums up the meaning of Purim. The English translation is this:

Blessed are You, Lord our God, King of the universe, who contends for us, judges our cause and avenges our wrong, who renders retribution to our mortal enemies and deals out punishment to our adversaries. Blessed are You, Lord, who on behalf of His people Israel deals out punishment to all their adversaries, God the Saviour. (*from 'Feasts and fasts of Israel', Hillel Avidan*)

The reading of the Megillah often takes on a pantomime atmosphere with hissing, booing and stamping of feet whenever the evil Haman is mentioned. Purim is the most secular of the Jewish festivals and although all its elements can be invested with religious meaning, most Jews simply want to enjoy themselves on this day. It is a time of feasting and drinking and although Judaism usually forbids excessive drinking it is encouraged at Purim as long as it is not likely to lead to accidents or immorality. Three-cornered cakes, stuffed with honey and poppy-seeds, are eaten to represent Haman's ears or pockets. It is a time for fancy dress and carnivals (see Fig. 2), the most famous being the Israeli national carnival held in Tel Aviv which has a big procession of floats through the streets. Children perform plays based on the Esther story and go round the houses collecting for charity. It is a time for giving presents to friends and neighbours and there is an obligation to share with the poor, either directly or by giving to charities.

Make sure you know
1 how many Jews died in the Holocaust
2 the name of at least one Nazi concentration camp where Jews were taken
3 the story of Purim

See if you understand
4 why Jews want to keep alive the memory of the Holocaust

Issues to discuss
5 The Jews have suffered because for a long time they have been without a homeland and been forced to settle in foreign countries. Why is it that many people do not want immigrants in their country? What benefits can immigrants often bring?
6 Are you convinced by any of the Jewish answers to the problem of suffering? What further thoughts have you got on this subject?

Further assignment
7 Write a poem entitled 'Holocaust'.

13 The Promised Land

Moses led the Jews towards the land of Canaan where their
ancestors had once lived. This was the Promised Land for which
they had left Egypt, 'the land flowing with milk and honey' (Exodus
3 verse 17) for which they had borne the hardships of the desert for
many years. Moses himself never entered the Promised Land but
looked out over it, across the blue waters of the Dead Sea, from the
heights of Mount Nebo. It was in this region that he died and was
buried.

When the Jews first infiltrated Canaan, they settled as scattered
tribes. It took the threat of a greater power, that of the Philistines
from the coastal plain, to forge them into a nation in the middle of
the 11th century BCE. It was because of the Philistines that this land
was called *Palestine*, a name which has often been used since. So
they united under King Saul, but it was his successor, David, who
was the greatest king of the Jews. He was a great warrior who put
down the Philistines, established Jerusalem as his capital city and
extended his control over the surrounding countries. But this kingdom did not remain intact, splitting in the 10th century into Judah in
the south and Israel in the north. They fell prey to the greater
powers: in 722 BCE the Northern Kingdom was destroyed by the
Assyrians and many Israelites were taken off to foreign parts; in 586
BCE Jerusalem, the capital of Judah, fell to the Babylonians and its
people were taken into exile.

This was a devastating blow to the morale of the people of Judah
for, despite the destruction of their northern sister and the warnings
of great prophets, they had believed that God would always protect
his holy city, built on Mount Zion, since it contained the Temple of
God. Even in exile they thought longingly of her:

By the rivers of Babylon we sat down and wept
when we remembered Zion.
There on the willow-trees
we hung up our harps,
for there those who carried us off
demanded music and singing,
and our captors called on us to be merry:
'Sing us one of the songs of Zion.'

How could we sing the Lord's song
in a foreign land?
If I forget you, O Jerusalem,
let my right hand wither away;
let my tongue cling to the roof of my mouth
if I do not remember you,
if I do not set Jerusalem
above my highest joy. (*Psalm 137 verses 1-6*)

Some Jews never returned to their homeland but set up Jewish communities all over the known world, in countries like Egypt, Syria and Greece. This is known as the Diaspora, or Dispersion of the Jews, and it is a movement which has continued into the 20th century. Others managed to return to Jerusalem and its small surrounding region of Judaea when Babylon was in turn subdued by the Persians fifty years later. They had maintained their religious traditions in exile and now they dedicated themselves anew to fulfil God's laws.

In 333 BCE the Persian empire fell to Alexander the Great of Greece and from then onwards Palestine was ruled by Hellenists until the Maccabean Wars in the 2nd century BCE which gained Jewish independence for nearly a hundred years (see chapter 10). Then in 63 BCE Pompey, the Roman commander, marched on Jerusalem, so beginning the era of Roman rule which was to last for nearly 700 years.

The Jews were fiercely nationalistic, resenting foreign domination, and the Great Revolt which broke out in 66 CE and quickly spread to all areas was not unexpected. Roman legions arrived and systematically crushed the centres of resistance until they came to Jerusalem itself. In the year 70 CE the siege was mounted which finally brought the city to its knees and ended in bloody defeat. The city was ransacked and hundreds of thousands of Jews were killed; but worst of all for the Jews, their holy Temple was destroyed by fire.

Some Jews still held out for a further three years against the might of Rome at a place called **Masada** in the barren Judaean Desert, overlooking the Dead Sea. This is a natural rock fortress, 900 feet high, where King Herod the Great had built palaces, fortifications, store houses and water cisterns during the previous century. At the beginning of the Great Revolt a group of freedom fighters, known as Zealots, killed the small Roman garrison stationed there and settled there themselves. They were joined by their families and refugees from other areas as they fell to the Roman army and finally by some who had escaped after the destruction of Jerusalem. A Roman army of 10 000 arrived at the end of 72 CE, determined to wipe out this last pocket of Jewish resistance. They built an enormous siege wall around Masada, over two miles long and linking together the eight army camps. They then set to work building a massive ramp up which they could drag their siege engines for an assault on the walls. The Jews resisted bravely but they were greatly outnumbered and they knew they were trapped. As you look down from the flat summit of Masada you can still see the square outlines of the Roman camps far below and the ramp, with its straight, sloping sides of a slightly lighter appearance than the golden mountain against which it leans. It is not hard to imagine the panic of the inhabitants as they watched the ramp getting higher and higher. When at last it was finished and the Jews realised they had no chance of escape they made a stunning decision. They decided that they would rather die a quick death as free people than surrender to the Romans. The next day, when the Romans breached the walls, they found that the 960 inhabitants, men, women and children, had committed mass suicide. This chilling story of nationalism and bravery stirs a chord in the heart of modern Jews. Masada has become a national shrine and place of pilgrimage, and there is a slogan: 'Masada shall not fall again.'

The Great Revolt had demonstrated the strong spirit of resistance among the Jews which the Romans could not allow to continue. They depopulated Jerusalem and established a standing army there. These measures led to one final revolt between 132-135 CE under Simon Bar Kochba who was regarded by many to be the Messiah. Once more the Romans subdued them with heavy casualties on both sides. The Emperor Hadrian now instituted anti-Jewish measures in Judaea. He called the country Syria Palestine and turned Jerusalem into a pagan city re-named Aelia Capitolina (Aelia being Hadrian's surname) and forbade Jews to enter it.

Jerusalem remained closed to the Jews for 150 years until pilgrims were allowed to visit it once more and gradually small groups of Jews settled there again. Apart from the few years when Bar Kochba had established himself there, the Jews were not masters of their capital city for 1900 years. Jerusalem remained under Roman rule until the 7th century and then came under successive Muslim empires until the 20th century, apart from the 12th-century Christian Crusader rule. In all this time a small Jewish community survived in Palestine, doggedly clinging to this land as their religious inheritance and keeping alive its language (Hebrew) and its culture.

Although the majority of Jews lived elsewhere, the Holy Land remained their spiritual home and some Jews even returned there in their old age to be buried in its soil. Their roots were never forgotten as they turned daily three times towards Jerusalem in prayer and annually declared at the climax of the Passover festival: 'Next year in Jerusalem'. During the Middle Ages many Jews left Europe to return to the four holy cities in Palestine: Jerusalem, Hebron, Tiberias and Safad. During the 19th century the Zionist movement

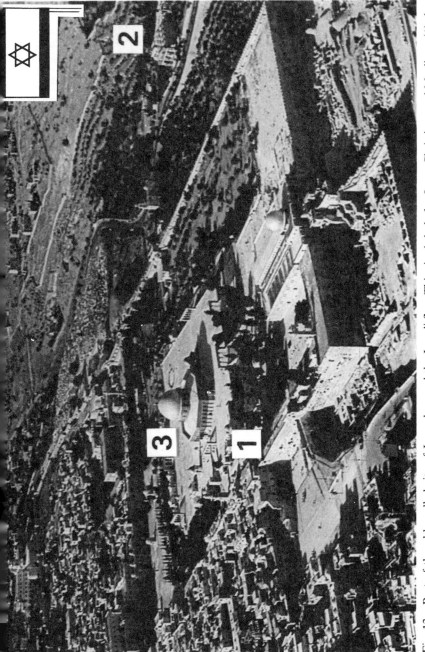

Fig. 13   Part of the old, walled city of Jerusalem and the Israeli flag. This city is holy for Jews, Christians and Muslims: (1) the Western Wall, all that remains standing of the Jewish Temple; (2) the Mount of Olives, where Jesus Christ was arrested the night before his crucifixion, (3) the Dome of the Rock, a magnificent mosque which dominates the original Temple Mount and marks the place from which Muhammad is said to have visited heaven.

developed which encouraged Jews to return to Palestine and buy land from the Arabs to set up new Jewish colonies there. It gave new hope to Jews in the anti-Semitic countries of Eastern Europe and inspired patriotism in Jews who were being assimilated into Western culture. Pioneers arrived ready to try their hand at agriculture and undergo great hardships. They began to use Hebrew as their common language. The first **kibbutz** was established in the early 20th century at Degania (meaning 'God's corn') on the southern tip of the Sea of Galilee. A kibbutz is a Jewish commune based on the socialist ideals of equality, collective ownership and communal living. All able-bodied men and women work and the income of the kibbutz goes into a common purse which is controlled democratically by its members. The first such experiments were so successful that there are now 229 kibbutzim (plural of kibbutz) with a total population of about 100 000 (roughly 3 per cent of the national population). Other types of co-operative villages were also set up, based on mutual help and co-operative bulk buying and selling but where individuals were responsible for their own plot of land which they owned and benefited from. These communities are more popular than the kibbutzim.

After the First World War (1914-18) Britain took control of Palestine and declared itself to be in favour of the establishment of a national home for the Jewish people in Palestine as long as this did not prejudice the rights of the Arabs there. The 1920s were relatively peaceful but Jewish immigration increased so much in the 1930s that the Arabs were alarmed when the Jews formed nearly a third of the population of Palestine. One of the reasons for this increase was the fanatical anti-Semitic policy of Hitler in Germany. In 1936 an Arab offensive broke out against Jewish settlers and lasted for two years. The British were unable to find a solution acceptable to both sides and were soon preoccupied with the Second World War (1939-45).

After the war Britain surrendered her control of Palestine and handed over the problem to the United Nations who recommended an equal partition of Palestine between its Arab and Jewish occupants. The Jews were ready to accept but the Arabs were not, and violence broke out. Surrounded as they were by seven Arab states, the Arabs saw no reason why they should lose their own land to an independent state of only 600 000 Jews. On the 14th May 1948 the Declaration of Independence was signed by David Ben-Gurion, the first Prime Minister of the new **State of Israel**.

The flag of Israel is white with a blue 'Magen David' (Shield of David), also known as the Star of David. It has a blue line above and below the star, representing the parallel lines on the Jewish prayer shawl. The origin of the symbol is unknown but the name for it goes back only to the 12th century CE. David's name was probably associated with it because he was the greatest Jewish king and inspires hope for their freedom and happiness. It is for this reason that it became a symbol of Zionism and so became adopted as the flag of the new State of Israel. Naturally it is well in evidence on Independence Day which is celebrated each year with parades, dancing and singing in the streets.

The State of Israel has survived against all odds and has continually grown in strength. Yet its history has been one of continual conflict with its Arab neighbours and unrest from the Arabs under Israeli rule, who now number a million. No sooner had independence been announced than they were invaded on all sides by Egypt, Syria, Lebanon, Jordan and Iraq. This War of Independence ended eight months later with an Israeli victory and the extension of its territory. From 1949-56 Israel remained the target of Arab terrorist attacks, especially from the Gaza Strip along the Mediterranean coast which housed 300 000 hostile Arab refugees who had fled from their homes in Israeli territory. This led to the Israelis attacking Gaza and another war in 1956 during which they routed the Egyptian forces in the Sinai. The superpowers of America and Russia now sided with Israel and Egypt respectively and supplied them with weapons. Fortunately the Six-Day War in June 1967 was short-lived. The Israelis were again victorious and to their great delight they captured the Old City of Jerusalem which had previously been in the Arab sector. The reunification of Jerusalem is celebrated annually on Jerusalem Day. The fourth war of 1973 is known as the Yom Kippur War because the Egyptians launched a surprise attack across the Suez Canal on this Jewish holy day. The war lasted for a month and once more the Israelis won, despite Egypt's initial success. Things began to look brighter in the late 70s when Egypt and Israel began negotiations with the help of the USA. President Sadat of Egypt made his historic visit to Jerusalem in 1980 and the road between the two countries was opened for the first time. Yet this only isolated Egypt from its Arab neighbours, and extremists on both Arab and Jewish sides continued to oppose more moderate peace agreements like the evacuation of Jewish settlers from the Sinai. Then in 1982 Israel invaded Lebanon, killing thousands of people, in an attempt to stamp out the strongholds of the Arab guerrilla movement, the Palestine Liberation Organisation.

To the Jews, Israel is not just any land but the Promised Land, given to them by God. Many Progressive Jews see the establishment of Israel as the dawn of the Messianic Age, the beginning of the Kingdom of God, the triumph of Judaism which has been awaited since biblical times. On the other hand, Orthodox Jews still await an individual Messiah and some ultra-Orthodox Jews living in Jerusalem dissociate themselves from the state, denouncing it as artificial. They live in Jerusalem because they believe that the Messiah will one day appear there, in the Holy City, to establish an age of peace for all mankind.

Make sure you know
1 how to draw the Shield (or Star) of David
2 the results of the Great Revolt
3 when the State of Israel was established

See if you understand
4 why Jerusalem remained the heart of Judaism, even when very few Jews lived there
5 what Masada symbolises for Jews
6 why the Jews feel the State of Israel has the right to exist

Further assignment
7 Organise a debate to put both sides of the Israeli/Arab conflict. The motion is 'This house believes that the Jews have a right to their Promised Land.'

List of Hebrew words

In the study of Judaism you will come across many Hebrew words. I have tried to use only the most important, or words which have no direct English equivalent. You may find Hebrew words spelt in a variety of ways in English. This is because Hebrew letters are different from ours and there are several ways of putting them into our Latin alphabet. This list does not include the names of festivals which are explained in the chart on page 9, but it has all other Hebrew words used in this book, with their meanings.

Pronunciation: 'ch' is never pronounced as in *ch*air but is a hard 'h' as in 'lo*ch*'.

Adonai	'my Lord' — used instead of saying God's name
Amidah	'standing' — name of the main Jewish prayer, said *standing* during services
Ashkenazi (pl. ___im)	'Germany' — came to refer to a Jew of Western, Central or Eastern Europe or a descendant in America, Asia or Australia
Bar Mitzvah	'son of the commandment' — ceremony marking a boy's coming of age in Judaism
Bat Mitzvah	'daughter of the commandment' — ceremony marking a girl's coming of age in Judaism
bimah	reading desk in the synagogue
chanukkiyah (pl. ___yot)	a modern name for the eight-branched candelabrum used at the festival of Chanukkah
charoset	sweet paste eaten at the Seder meal at Passover
Diaspora	dispersion of Jews outside Israel
Gemara	'completion' — Jewish scripture, part of the Talmud, consisting of commentary on the Mishnah
Haggadah	'telling' — book containing the ritual for the Seder meal, *retelling* the events of the exodus
halakah	'path' – the consensus of Jewish laws, emerging from the Talmud
Hallel	Psalms of praise, nos. 113-118
havdalah	'separation' — ceremony to mark the end of festivals, particularly the Sabbath
kaddish	'sanctification' — a prayer recited by mourners of the dead

Ketuvim	the 'Writings' — name for the last section of the Hebrew Bible
kibbutz (pl. ___zim)	a village commune
kosher	'fit', 'proper' — adj. to describe something that is *suitable* for use according to Jewish regulations, e.g. food
matzot (pl.)	unleavened bread
Megillah	'a scroll' — used of five books of the Hebrew Bible, e.g. Book of Esther
menorah	candelabrum, particularly the seven-branched menorah which is the most ancient sign of Judaism
Messiah (adj. Messianic)	'anointed one' — Jewish idea of a saviour to be sent by God
mezuzah	'doorpost' — rolled parchment in a case fixed to a *doorpost*
minyan	minimum of 10 adult males to form a congregation
Mishnah	'repetition', 'review' — Jewish scripture, a written record of the Oral Tradition
mohel	circumciser
Neviim	the 'Prophets' — name of the second section of the Hebrew Bible
Rabbenu	'our teacher' (see below)
rabbi	theologian, teacher
Sabbath (or Shabbat)	'to cease' - last day of the week, a holy day of *rest*
sandek	godfather who holds the baby in his lap for circumcision
Seder	'order' — the ritualised Passover meal
Sephardi (pl. ___im)	'Spain' — a Jew who originated from the *Iberian* peninsula
shalom	'peace' — common Jewish greeting
Shema	'hear' — the first word of, and hence the name for, some passages of scripture recited frequently by Jews and which summarise their belief in God
shofar	ram's horn, blown before and during the festival of Rosh Hashanah and at the end of Yom Kippur
Siddur	'order', 'arrangement' — name of the Jewish prayer book
sukkah (pl. sukkot)	booth, tabernacle or hut used at the festival of Sukkot
Talmud	'to study' — Jewish scripture, consisting of the Mishnah and Gemara
tallit	prayer shawl
Tefillah	'prayer' — another title for the Amidah
tefillin	'prayers' — also called phylacteries, small boxes containing scriptures, worn by men at morning prayer
Tenach	name for the Hebrew Bible, the word comes from the Hebrew letters T,N and K, standing for Torah, Neviim and Ketuvim

| Torah | 'teaching' — strictly it refers to the first part of the Hebrew Bible, the Pentateuch, but it is sometimes used for the entire Hebrew scriptures |
| Yhwh | the Hebrew name for God, too holy to be spoken by Jews, but pronounced as either Yahweh or Jehovah by gentiles |

Useful addresses

Education Officer,
Central Jewish Lecture and Information Committee,
Board of Deputies of British Jews,
Woburn House, Upper Woburn Place,
London WC1 0EP

The Information Department,
Embassy of Israel,
2 Palace Green, London W8 4QB,
Tel. 01-937 8050

Israel Government Tourist Office,
59 St James's Street, London SW1

Jewish Education Bureau,
8 Westcombe Avenue, Leeds LS8 2BS

JNF Publishing Company,
Harold Poster House,
Kingsbury Circle, London NW9 9SP

Study Centre for Christian-Jewish Relations,
17 Chepstow Villas, London W11 3DZ

Index